The Complete Country Dance Tunes

from

Playford's Dancing Master

(1651 – ca.1728)

EDITED BY JEREMY BARLOW

FABER MUSIC LIMITED, LONDON

To my colleagues in the Broadside Band:
Alastair McLachlan, Rosemary Thorndycraft and George Weigand

© 1985 by Faber Music Ltd
First published in 1985 by Faber Music Ltd
3 Queen Square London WC1N 3AU
Music drawn by Ronald Finch
Cover design by M & S Tucker
Printed in England by Caligraving Ltd
All rights reserved

Cover illustration: seventh edition, 1686,
title page engraving

The editor has made a record with the Broadside Band of music from the first edition of *The Dancing Master* using
instruments of the period: *Country Dances from John Playford's English Dancing Master 1651* (Harmonia Mundi HM 1109).
Several more tunes from *The Dancing Master* are included on two earlier records by the Broadside Band: *Popular Tunes in
17th Century England* (HM 1039) and *The Beggar's Opera: original songs and airs* with Patrizia Kwella (soprano) and
Paul Elliott (tenor) (HM 1071).

Contents

Preface

The eighteen successive editions of *The Dancing Master*, consisting of tunes and dance instructions for country dancing, were originally published between 1651 and about 1728, and together constitute the most important source of popular instrumental tunes to be found in England during that period. John Playford (1623–1686) published the first seven editions between 1651 and 1686 (calling the book *The English Dancing Master* for the 1651 edition only). His son Henry Playford (c.1657–c.1707) published the eighth to twelfth editions (1690–1703) and John Young (fl.1698–1732) the remaining six (1706–c.1728). In addition, Young published two separate collections of country dances, not included here, called the *Second Volume* and *Third Volume* of *The Dancing Master* (not to be confused with *The Second Part of The Dancing Master*, which is a supplement to the ninth edition; see p.7).

The 105 tunes in the first edition have been reprinted in recent times (see p.11), but the 430 tunes added in the later editions and supplements have only been available, if at all, scattered amongst various anthologies. This book presents, in modern notation, all the tunes for country dancing from the original editions, together with the many additions, omissions and alterations that occurred as the editions progressed.

Jeremy Barlow

Acknowledgements

First of all I must thank Margaret Dean-Smith and Tom Cook. Margaret Dean-Smith's book and articles (see p.11) have been a most useful source of information, and Tom Cook's unpublished work 'The Assembly' (see p.12) has been an invaluable means of checking aspects of my work. Both have been generous with their time in answering my queries. I would like to thank the librarians and staff of The British Library, Dundee District Library, Glasgow University Library, the Mitchell Library, Glasgow, and the Vaughan Williams Memorial Library, Cecil Sharp House, for their assistance and for allowing copies of *The Dancing Master* in their keeping to be used in preparing this edition. The British Library and the Vaughan Williams Memorial Library have kindly allowed their copies to be used for the plates.

How the book is organised

As the eighteen editions of *The Dancing Master* succeeded each other, changes were made not only to the tunes, but also to almost every aspect of the musical notation, including clefs, key and time signatures, barlines, slurs, beams, note values and coloration, and accidentals (see plates 4–6).

The section below summarises the way in which each edition was organised, notated and altered from earlier editions. The commentary (pp.121–127) gives for each tune the edition(s) in which it was found, the original time signature, misprints, ambiguities, exceptional changes between editions and other information which would make the music too cluttered. The title index (pp.132–136) shows alongside the spelling and tune no. in this edition, the spelling and page or tune number of each title from its earliest edition. Also included are a tune index (pp.129–131), a chart of libraries containing editions of *The Dancing Master* (p.13) and a short bibliography of sources of further information on John Playford and *The Dancing Master* (pp.11–12).

The editions and their musical characteristics[1]

The figure before the date of each edition and supplement below is used in the music and commentary for reference (see pp.8 and 121); the library and catalogue number indicate the copy used in preparing this book.

1   1651   First edition   Vaughan Williams Memorial Library, Cecil Sharp House, London QS 35.3 2245
The only edition to be called *The English Dancing Master*. The dances are arranged in apparently random order. The treble clef is used in its modern position on the stave, and also placed a third lower,[2] centred on the lowest stave line (see plate 4). The choice of clef is determined by the range of the tune and the customary avoidance of leger lines wherever possible. On the few occasions when a leger line is needed it is either very indistinct (nos. 13 and 60) or simply omitted (the highest notes in nos. 67 and 88). No single barlines are used except sometimes after an opening upbeat, or occasionally to separate first and second time endings; double bars are plain, without dots. The tunes in 6/4 and 3/4 are all in black notation[3] and use either **C** or **₵** for a time signature. The choice does not appear to have any significance and it is in any case often hard to distinguish between the two signs, because the stave line going through **C** is of variable length **€ € €**. The common time tunes use white instead of black minims and either **₡** or **Ɖ**. Here there is a clear difference in meaning, **Ɖ** signifying a much faster tempo than **₡**.[4] The edition contains many misprints. No instruments are specified, but in Playford's *A Musicall Banquet*, also of 1651, *The English Dancing Master* is advertised '. . . to be played on the Treble Violl or Violin'.

2   1652   Second edition   The British Library K.1.a.9
This and all remaining editions are called *The Dancing Master*. '. . . to be playd on the Treble Violin' is added to the title page. The dances are rearranged into rough alphabetical order of title (correct to the first letter only). A few more tunes now use the treble clef in its modern position and leger lines are used clearly. **C** is changed to **₵** and vice versa for some of the triple time tunes. There does not appear to be any significance in these changes (see above). The tie sign is modernised from ⌢ to ⌒. The notation otherwise remains the same as in the first edition. Tunes are often altered and although some misprints in the first edition are corrected, plenty of new mistakes are introduced, in spite of the claim on the title page 'The second Edition, Enlarged and Corrected from many grosse Errors which were in the former Edition.' Two dances from the first edition are omitted.

3   [1657] and 1665   Third edition[5]   Glasgow University Library GUL.Q.c.85 and The British Library K.1.a.10
The dances from the second edition are kept in the same order (a few are omitted). New dances are added at the end. Bar lines are introduced for all tunes (see plate 5) distinguishing 3/4 from 6/4, but not 6/4 from 9/4. Tunes in 9/4 are barred in 6/4. This demonstrates the slightly different function of the barline in its early use: an aid to visual clarity and not necessarily an indication of the strong beats. As John Playford states in his Preface '. . . And for the more easie playing of the Tunes, they are barred every Semibrief'. Double bars now have dots :||: , but final bars do not. The **C** and **₵** time signatures are replaced by **3** for most 3/4 and 6/4 tunes. White

---

[1] This section concentrates on musical rather than bibliographical details and is intended to be complementary as far as possible to the bibliographical section on the editions in the *Dean-Smith Facsimile* (see p.11).

[2] The clef known as the French violin clef.

[3] Playford's *A brief Introduction to the Skill of Musick*, fourth edition, 1664, states:

> This swifter *Triple time* is sometimes prick'd in *Black* Notes, which *Black* Note is of the same Measure with the *Minim* in the foregoing Example, but is seldom used, because the *Minims* are the same and serve as well.

(see also footnote on p.6)

[4] Op. cit., seventh edition, 1674, states:

> Note, that when this Common Mood *is reversed to* **Ɖ**, *it is to signifie, that the* Time *of that Lesson or Song, before which it is so set, is to be Play'd or Sung as swift again as the usual Measure.*

The twelfth edition, 1694, adds 'The *French Mark* for this retorted *Time* is a large Figure of **2** '.

[5] See *Dean-Smith Facsimile*. Playford advertised a new edition in 1657, yet all surviving copies of the third edition are dated 1665. The Glasgow University copy however has a different supplement (3A), as well as a few differences in the main body of the book, and is therefore assumed to be a copy of the 1657 printing, even though it lacks the title page and date.

notation replaces black in about half of the 3/4 and 6/4 tunes; this replacement continues bit by bit in subsequent editions, until the eleventh.[6] Slurs are used for the first time.

As in the second edition, the tunes are frequently altered. Some mistakes are corrected, but again new errors are introduced. Almost all the changes occur in the earlier printing; exceptions are identified in the text or commentary.

3A [1657] Glasgow University Library GUL.Q.c.85
Entitled 'The Tunes *of the French Dances and other New* Tunes *for the* TREBLE-VIOLIN.', this is included at the end of the third edition, without an index (see 3B below). The title page has an illustration of the violin and its tuning.

3B 1665 The British Library K.1.a.10
This supplement has the same title as 3A, but the contents differ considerably. An index is provided at the front of the book, immediately after the index for the third edition itself. Neither 3A nor 3B include dance instructions. The 'other New Tunes' from each supplement have been included here, but the French dances (mostly courantes) have been omitted, apart from one or two with a country dance character. These supplements appear to have given John Playford the idea for *Apollo's Banquet*, which additionally includes instructions on the rudiments of music and playing the violin. Some of the tunes from 3A and 3B reappear with dance instructions in later editions of *The Dancing Master*.

4 1670 Fourth edition The British Library K.1.a.11
The order of the dances is rearranged according to dance type, starting with round dances and ending with longways and figure dances. This principle is adhered to for all the remaining editions.

Alternative titles are introduced for several of the dances. The first use of $\mathbf{C}\,3$ and $\mathbf{\mathe{C}\!\!\!|\,3}$ is found for a few 6/4 tunes, for no apparent reason. Once again there are many alterations and corrections, but this time fewer new mistakes are introduced. A few dances from previous editions are omitted.

5 1675 Fifth edition The British Library K.1.a.12
Little change; lightly edited with few new mistakes.

6 1679 Sixth edition The British Library K.1.a.12*
Little change.

6A 1679 The British Library K.1.a.12*
'A *Supplement* to The *Dancing-Master* of new Dances,

never Printed before.' Included at the end of the sixth edition, this contains the first example in *The Dancing Master* of a correctly barred 9/4 tune, no. 233 (time signature $\mathbf{C}\,3$ as for new 6/4 tunes). All the dances are incorporated into the seventh edition.

7 1686 Seventh edition The British Library K.1.a.14
Although John Playford had retired in 1684, this edition still bears his imprint. The title page has a new illustration (see cover). Altogether this is more strongly edited than the fifth and sixth editions, with several alterations and some new mistakes.

7A [1687] The British Library K.1.a.14
'TUNES *of other* Country-Dances *added to this Book.*' This is included at the end of one of the two copies of the seventh edition in the British Library. The tunes have no dance instructions; about one third reappear with dances in later editions.

7B [1688] The British Library K.1.a.14
'A *new Additional Sheet to the* DANCING-MASTER'. This and all the remaining supplements include dance instructions.

7C [1689] The British Library K.1.a.14
'A *new Addition to the* DANCING-MASTER'. The dances from 7B and 7C are incorporated into the eighth edition. The dates of these three supplements (7A, 7B, 7C) are based on the order in which they appear at the end of the seventh edition and the possibility that one was issued each year between the publication of the seventh and eighth editions. Advertisements at the end of the supplements mention Henry Playford's name for the first time.

8 1690 Eighth edition The British Library K.1.a.15
The first edition to be published under Henry Playford's name. The editing is light and there are few corrections or new mistakes, apart from the use of $\mathbf{C}\,3$ for most 6/4 and 3/4 tunes throughout the book. There is some rearrangement of order and Henry Playford states in his preface that he has 'left out some of the old *Dances*, but in their place added twice as many new ones never before printed'.

9 1695 Ninth edition The British Library K.1.a.16
Further rearrangement of order, some alterations and corrections to the tunes, and not too many new misprints. The edition contains the first use in *The Dancing Master* of a 6/4 time signature instead of $\mathbf{C}\,3$. The preface states '. . . most of the *Tunes* being within the compass of the *Flute*.' The word 'flute' by itself at this time meant 'recorder'; the statement reflects the rapidly growing popularity of the baroque instrument. A considerable number of

---

[6] The commentary indicates the edition in which each tune originally notated in black notation is changed to white.

earlier dances, particularly those going back to the first edition, are left out.

9A 1696 The British Library K.1.a.16
'The second Part of the Dancing Master[7] . . . for the *Violin* or *Flute* . . . Printed for *Henry Playford* at his Shop . . . Where both Parts are to be had bound together at 3s. Or this Second Part stitch'd at 1s.' Although called Part II and given a separate title page, this is really just another supplement. The fact that it could be bought separately from the ninth and tenth editions perhaps indicates that Henry Playford was worried about the price of the two together (see also his stress on value for money in the eleventh edition below). Unlike his father, Henry Playford had to contend with increasing competition from other music publishers. **2** is used for the first time as a time signature, having the same meaning as 𝔇 (see fn 4 p.5). Time signatures are omitted in several new tunes, both in this and subsequent editions, although the omissions are almost always rectified later. The dances from Part II and its additional supplements are not included as part of the tenth edition (see 9B below), but do become incorporated into the main body of the eleventh edition. In his short preface, Henry Playford states concerning the dance instructions that 'most of them are made by Mr. *Beveredge* and the rest by other Eminent Masters'.

9B 1698 The British Library K.1.a.18
'The Second Part of the Dancing Master . . . The Second Edition, with Additions.' The first eight pages of the additions are to be found in the Mitchell Library, Glasgow copy with the heading '*An Additional Sheet of New Dances for the* Second Part *of the* Country-Dancing-Master.' It might be thought that this edition was intended as a supplement to the tenth edition, also published in 1698, but Margaret Dean-Smith states[8] that 9B was advertised in February 1698 whereas the tenth edition was not advertised until the summer. However, the copy of the tenth edition at the Vaughan Williams Memorial Library has at the end 9B, 9C and 9D, without title page, preface or any headings, but with the page numbers for these supplements starting at page 1.

9C [1698] The British Library K.1.a.18
No heading, but the page numbers indicate that the dances in this section were probably added separately at some point. The first edition of Part II (9A) is paginated 1–24 and the additional pages in 9B run from 25–36. This section starts again at p.25 and again runs through to p.36. The duplicated page numbers are given asterisks in Playford's index.

7 Not to be confused with *The Second Volume of The Dancing Master* (see p.4).

8 *Dean-Smith Facsimile* (see p.11).

9D [1698] The British Library K.1.a.18
'*An Additional Sheet to the* Second Part *of the* Dancing-Master.' Starts at p.37.

10 1698 Tenth edition The British Library K.1.a.17
There are few changes from the ninth edition, apart from time signatures. 𝗖3 becomes ₵3 in several tunes, 6/4 in a few others. ₵ is sometimes reversed to 𝔇. From the character of the tunes remaining in ₵, it would appear that this time signature now often indicates a slower tempo than in earlier editions.

11 1701 Eleventh edition The British Library K.1.b.1
'. . . *The whole Printed in the New* Character.' This refers to the use of 'tied note' notation, in which quavers and smaller note values are grouped by their beams into pairs or larger groupings. At the same time, the last remaining tunes in black notation are changed to white. Henry Playford states

'To all *Lovers of* Country Dancing, and the *Pleasing Recreation of Playing on a* Violin or Flute. /Gentlemen,/ *This* Country-Dance *Book, with many Additions of Excellent new* Dances *us'd at Court, and Play-Houses, and other Publick Meetings, is by great Labour and a Greater Charge, at last done in the New Tied Note, after the manner of Pricking; more intelligible than ever, being the* Eleventh *Edition, containing double the Number of* Dances *that was in the former, and the Price advanced 6d. only, which is 3s. for the Book compleat.'*

There are more changes to time signatures: 6/4, 3/4 and **3i** are all used for tunes barred as 6/4, and both 3/4 and **3i** are used for tunes barred as 3/4. Some 6/4 time signatures are changed to 3/2 for appropriate tunes. There are a few changes in the order of the dances, and those from Part II and its supplements are incorporated before the new dances. This is the last edition to omit a substantial number of dances from previous editions.

11A 1702 Dundee District Library, Wighton Collection G.92404H
'TWENTY FOUR NEW COUNTRY DANCES. Printed by *William Pearson* for *Henry Playford* . . . 1702.' The copy of the eleventh edition in the above collection has this supplement, all of which is incorporated in the twelfth edition.

12 1703 Twelfth edition The British Library K.1.b.2
'. . . *containing above 350 of the choicest* Old *and* New Tunes *now used at Court, and other Publick Places*'. This edition reverts to the old notation with separate tails for all quavers and smaller note values. It is nevertheless carefully edited, and for once the often

repeated claim 'much more Correct than any former Editions' has some validity. Considerable care is taken over time signatures, accidentals, and in particular, the use of slurs. The use of the 6/4 time signature becomes more prevalent and more tunes in 3/2 now have the correct time signature. Several tunes in 3/4 are changed to 6/4 and rebarred accordingly. Most tunes in 9/4 now have the correct barring.

13 1706 Thirteenth edition Vaughan Williams Memorial Library, Cecil Sharp House, London QS 35.4 2257
'. . . done in the New Ty'd-Note and much more Correct than any former Editions.' The first edition to be published by John Young. The tied note notation is reintroduced and used for all remaining editions. Here the claim 'much more Correct' is not justified. The editor or printer appears to have used a copy of the eleventh edition for reference because several of the corrections in the twelfth edition are ignored.

14 1709 Fourteenth edition Vaughan Williams Memorial Library, Cecil Sharp House, London QS 35.4 2212
Carefully edited, recorrecting most of the errors in the thirteenth edition. There are some changes of order in the dances and a few from previous editions are omitted. This and the next two editions are musically the most accurate.

15 1713 Fifteenth edition The British Library K.1.b.3
Another carefully produced edition with little change

from the fourteenth. On the title page the availability of the *Second Volume* is mentioned (see p.4), and also 'the Basses to all the Dances contain'd in this Volume'. No copy of the basses has been found.

16 1716 Sixteenth edition The British Library K.1.b.4
Little change.

17 1721 Seventeenth edition The British Library K.1.b.6
Several tunes formerly in C or G are transposed, mostly up a tone. There are also a number of melodic changes, with simple divisions and changes to cadential phrases. More new mistakes are introduced than in the previous three editions.

18 c.1728[8] Eighteenth edition The British Library   Hirsch M.1382
A new illustration on the title page shows a trio (violin, oboe and bassoon) accompanying the dancers (see plate 2). There are a few changes to the spelling of titles; otherwise this is almost identical to the seventeenth edition with few corrections and few new mistakes.

[8] Precise date unknown. The British Library gives c.1725, but the *Dean-Smith Facsimile* (see p.11) suggests a date later than 1728. It cannot have been published later than 1732, the year of John Young's death.

Editorial method in the music

A tune as printed in this book consists of the earliest version in *The Dancing Master*, but incorporating corrections made in later editions. Misprints are shown in the commentary. Variants from later editions are printed in small type, unless there are so many that the whole tune has to be printed again. However, the distinction between misprint and variant is not always clear cut and there are cases where a probable misprint makes musical sense and has even become known as a variant. For example, the second strain of 'Newcastle' (no.67) is often played today with a top g" in bar 10 instead of the corrected a" found in the second edition onwards (see p.5). Wherever possible, ambiguities of this

sort have been presented in the music and not hidden away in the commentary. A few tunes remain corrupt throughout the original editions, and where a remedy has not been found these tunes have been printed as they stand.

The numbers placed next to variants refer to the editions in which those variants occur (see the previous section for the numbering of the editions and supplements):
12 means 'occurs in the twelfth edition only'.
12+ means 'occurs in the twelfth edition and all the remaining editions which contain that tune' (the commentary indicates which editions contain each tune).

-12 means 'occurs in all editions which contain the tune, up to and including the twelfth edition'.

Variant slurs, barlines and ties are dotted. Where plain and dotted slurs occur simultaneously ⌢⌢ the plain slurs occur in all editions before the edition with the variant reading.

Editorial suggestions are in square brackets, editorial barlines are shortened, and editorial ties marked ⌢ (there are no editorial slurs). The treble clef centred on the lowest stave (see p.5) found in the first two editions is raised to its modern position and the music transposed accordingly (see commentary).

Time signatures are modernised and changes indicated in the following way: **3**, **3i** and 3/4 are shown as 3/4 only when barred as 3/4 in the original editions (there are many instances of tunes barred as 6/4 with, at various times, **3**, **3i** or 3/4 as a time signature, but in almost all these cases the time signature becomes altered to 6/4 in later editions). **D** and **2** are retained from the original editions because of their special meaning (see p.5). Alterations between **C** and **D**, and in barring from from 3/4 to 6/4 are shown in the music because of their possible relevance to tempo; other changes to time signatures and barring which do not form part of the overall changes between editions mentioned in the previous section are shown in the commentary. Those tunes in early editions which do not survive into the editions with modern time signatures have their time signatures modernised without comment unless necessary.

Original note values have been retained (for comments on the black notation used in the first ten editions, see p.5). First and second time bars and the values of final notes are adjusted without comment unless there is some ambiguity. The *petite reprise* sign **:S:** indicates a repeat from the next double bar back to the sign. It has been retained from the original editions for repeats of part of a strain, but omitted when it comes over a double bar and can therefore be replaced with a double bar repeat sign. Repeats are indicated for all strains unless the dance instructions state unequivocally that a strain is to be played once only.[1]

The use of accidentals is modernised and redundant accidentals eliminated without comment unless necessary. (In the original editions, as in other music of the period, naturalised flats are indicated with a sharp sign and vice versa.)

Modern beaming conventions have been used. The way in which quavers and semiquavers are linked in the 'tied note' editions (11, 13–18) appears to result from the problem of linking notes with movable type (which involves a separate piece of type for each note), rather than from an intention to indicate bowing or articulation.[2] Quavers tend to be linked in groups of more than two when the music is not too angular, i.e. on repeated notes or on adjacent notes moving in the same direction.

The words 'separate entry' above an alternative title mean that the tune re-enters under that title in the edition or supplement indicated. Tunes are arranged in alphabetical order of title within each edition (see the notes on editions 1, 3 and 4 for the various arrangements of order used in the original editions, and also the title index, which gives the page or tune no. from the edition in which a title first appears). Names prefixed by Mr. are placed according to the name, since the use of Mr. is not consistent in the original editions. Spellings tend to become modernised and standardised as the editions progress, but there is much variety, both between the index and the dance heading (see the title index), and between one edition and another. The latest or most consistent spellings from the original editions have been used for names; other words have been modernised (for ease of alphabetical reference) unless in a dialect or of unclear meaning. The earliest spelling for each title is given in the title index. The following terms have been standardised:

original spellings	*standardised*
Ayre	air
Bore, Boree	Bourrée
Entrey	Entrée
Figgary, Fagary, Vegarie, Vagarie	vagary
Gavot	Gavotte
Jeg, Jegge, Jigg, Jigge	Jig
Magot, Magott, Maggott	maggot
Paspe, Pasbe	Passepied
Rigadoon	Rigaudon

Capitalisation in the titles has been kept to a minimum, with a distinction made between names

---

[1] A double bar, with or without dots (see plates 4–6), did not necessarily indicate a repeat, although the dance instructions usually imply repeats of each strain. Playford's *An Introduction to the Skill of Musick*, twelfth edition, 1694 (rewritten by Purcell), states:

> The *double Bars* are set to divide the several *Strains* or *Stanzas* of the *Songs* and *Lessons*; and are thus made :‖: . A repeat is marked thus **S** [in this edition **:S:**] and is used to signifie, that such a part of a Song or Lesson must be played or sung over again from the Note over which it is placed.

[2] It might be considered significant that the twelfth edition, which reverts to the non-tied beams of editions 1–10 and can therefore only indicate articulation through the use of slurs, is the edition in which slurs are most carefully edited. A comparison of the eleventh and twelfth editions shows the following: in the eleventh edition slurs over pairs of notes (by far the most common slurring throughout *The Dancing Master*) coincide usually but not invariably with notes beamed in pairs. But there are many notes beamed in pairs in the eleventh edition which are not slurred in the twelfth. Notes beamed in groups of four are usually left unslurred, although there are a few instances of slurs over two pairs of notes with beams across all four ♫♫ . Most of the notes beamed in fours in the eleventh edition remain unslurred in the twelfth; new slurs introduced in such cases are all in pairs.

relating to a specific musical form or dance, *Minuet, Bourrée* etc. (capitalised) and terms either of a more general nature, *air, dance, country dance, figure dance* etc. or without any musical or dance significance, *delight, frolic, maggot, vagary* etc. (uncapitalised). In the original editions nouns, but not other parts of speech, tend to be capitalised, although this system is not followed consistently. From the fourth edition onwards names of people and places become italicised with increasing frequency; they are capitalised in this book.

Performance

The following remarks are derived from the few clues about the performance of music for country dances which can be found through examining and comparing the eighteen editions of *The Dancing Master*.

It must first be emphasised that variant notes, rhythms, accidentals, key signatures and time signatures can, in spite of their smaller size, be as important as the 'main' notation (see p.8). Accidentals were marked with increasing care as the editions progressed (particularly from the twelfth edition onwards), reflecting the gradual disappearance of the use of *musica ficta*, a renaissance practice which gave the performer licence to introduce accidentals in certain places where none had been written, depending on the melodic and harmonic context; melodically *musica ficta* was used mainly to sharpen leading notes at cadences and to avoid the interval of the augmented fourth, but its application was also partly a matter of individual taste and expression.[1]

The way in which tunes were changed from the minor to major mode and vice-versa is intriguing. Some of the changes may simply have been corrections, others the result of editorial taste. When one takes into account sources of the tunes outside *The Dancing Master* there can be no doubt that a flexible attitude existed towards the modality of popular tunes in the 17th century.

The many rhythmic variants reveal a flexibility in rhythmic interpretation too. It should be noted that quavers were often played unequally, according to the convention of *notes inégales* which is demonstrated in *The Dancing Master* when ♫ is replaced by ♪. in a later edition.

Most of the tunes would have been played through several times when used for country dancing, as the dance instructions show. The variants sometimes indicate the style of divisions which might have been extemporised or worked out on the repeats (see p.9 for remarks on repeats).

Instruments mentioned in connection with the original editions are the treble viol (first edition only, see p.5), the violin (first edition onwards) and the recorder (ninth edition onwards, see p.6), but the tunes may not have been associated with any of those instruments, or indeed with country dancing, before appearing in *The Dancing Master*. The baroque oboe and bassoon are illustrated on the title page to the eighteenth edition (see plate 2); both had become familiar in England at the same time as the baroque recorder, during the last twenty years of the 17th century. The baroque flute, although it appears to have been developed in France alongside the recorder, oboe and bassoon, took much longer to catch on in England and did not establish itself firmly until the 1720s, the time of the last two editions.

All the tunes have strong harmonic implications, but many stand up well without accompaniment and were often played that way for dancing by violin, kit fiddle or pipe and tabor. Nevertheless, several tunes in the later editions, particularly those which modulate, do need harmonic support. Apart from the character of the tunes themselves, there are three bits of evidence in *The Dancing Master* to suggest that accompaniment became a more usual practice in the music for country dancing after the beginning of the 18th century. First, the basses to the tunes are mentioned as being available in the fifteenth and later editions (1713 onwards). Secondly, the title page illustration to the eighteenth edition (c.1728) (see above) shows three musicians playing for the dancers, and thirdly, the dance instructions to 'Joan Sanderson' (no.247) refer to 'the Musician' in the seventh to tenth editions, but to 'the Musicians' from the eleventh edition (1701) onwards. However, *The Dancing Master* is primarily a dance instruction book, and social dances continued to be taught by the dancing master with his fiddle for two hundred years or more after the publication of *The English Dancing Master* in 1651.

Although the basses to the fifteenth and later

[1] For a clear exposition of the practice of *musica ficta*, see the article by Nicholas Routley, 'A practical guide to *musica ficta*' in *Early Music*, Vol. 13 no. 1, February 1985, pp.59–71.

editions have not been found, it is likely that they would have been harmonically and rhythmically simple for most of the two-in-a-bar tunes; similar in style perhaps to those found in, for example, John Playford's *The Division Violin* (1684 and later) and John Gay's *The Beggar's Opera* (third edition, 1729, with basses by J. C. Pepusch). Both works contain tunes from *The Dancing Master* and are available in modern editions.[2] The longer, more developed pieces by Purcell and his contemporaries used in the later editions can often be found with basses in theatre, song and keyboard collections of the period, but dance musicians may not have had access to these sources, or necessarily have considered them suitable for use in country dance accompaniment.

[2] *The Division Violin* Facsimile edition with introductory notes and a realisation of the ground basses by Margaret Gilmore, London (1982).
The Beggar's Opera Edited by Edgar V. Roberts, music edited by Edward Smith, Nebraska (1968) and London (1969).
– with an introduction by Oswald Doughty and a facsimile of the music for the overture and songs from the 1729 edition, New York (1973).
– with accompaniments arranged for two oboes, strings and continuo, using the basses from the 1729 edition and the evidence of surviving ballad opera scores, by Jeremy Barlow and John Eliot Gardiner, London (1983).

Sources of information relating to John Playford and *The Dancing Master*

Books

DEAN-SMITH, MARGARET *Playford's English Dancing Master 1651 A Facsimile Reprint with an Introduction, Bibliography and Notes*, London (1957) **referred to in this edition as the *Dean-Smith Facsimile*.**
MELLOR, HUGH and BRIDGEWATER, LESLIE *John Playford's The English Dancing Master* with the text reset and the music transcribed into modern notation from the original 1651 edition, and with prefaces on the dances and music by Hugh Mellor and Leslie Bridgewater respectively, London (1933); reprinted New York (n.d.); reprinted London (1984).

Articles

ANON. 'English Country Dances: A Summary of Views as to Their Nature and Origin' *Journal of the English Folk Dance Society*, 2nd series, No.1 (1927), pp.52–56.
CORAL, L. 'A John Playford Advertisement' *Royal Musical Association Research Chronicle*, Vol.V (1965), p.1.
CUNNINGHAM, J. P. 'The Country Dance – Early References' *Journal of the English Folk Dance and Song Society*, Vol.IX, No.3 (1962), pp.148–154.
DEAN-SMITH, MARGARET 'English Tunes Common to Playford's *Dancing Master*, the Keyboard Books and Traditional Songs and Dances' *Proceedings of The Royal Musical Association*, Vol.LXXIX (1952–3), illustrated frontispiece, pp.1–17.
– 'Playford': articles on members of the family in *Die Musik in Geschichte und Gegenwart*, Kassel and Basle (1962).

– 'Playford': articles on members of the family in *The New Grove Dictionary of Music and Musicians*, London (1980).
DEAN-SMITH, MARGARET and NICOL, E. J. 'The Dancing Master 1651–1728': Part 1. [Bibliography]; Part 2. 'Country Dance and Revelry before 1651'; Part 3. 'Our Country Dances' *Journal of the English Folk Dance and Song Society*, Vol.IV, No.4 (1943), pp.131–145; Vol.IV, No.5 (1944), pp.167–179; Vol.IV, No.6 (1945), pp.211–231.
GILCHRIST, ANNE G. 'Some Additional Notes on the Traditional History of Certain Ballad-Tunes in *The Dancing Master* (1650)' *Journal of The English Folk Dance and Song Society*, Vol.III, No.4 (1939), pp.274–280.
KIDSON, FRANK 'John Playford and Seventeenth Century Music Publishing' *The Musical Quarterly*, Vol.IV, No.4 (1918), pp.516–34.
SQUIRE, W. BARCLAY 'John Playford' *Music & Letters*, Vol.IV, No.3 (1923), pp.261–265.
TEMPERLEY, NICHOLAS 'John Playford and the Stationers' Company' *Music & Letters*, Vol.LIV (1973), p.203.
THURSTON, HUGH 'The Development of the Country Dance as Revealed in Printed Sources' *Journal of the English Folk Dance and Song Society*, Vol.VII, No.1 (1952), pp.29–35.
WELLS, EVELYN K. 'Playford Tunes and Broadside Ballads': Part 1. '*The Dancing Master* and its Tunes'; Parts 2 and 3. 'A List of Broadside Ballads set to the Tunes of *The Dancing Master* of 1650' *Journal of the English Folk Dance and Song Society*, Vol.III, No.2

(1937), pp.81–92; Vol.III, No.3 (1938), pp.195–202; Vol.III, No.4 (1939), pp.259–273.

WOOD, MELUSINE 'English Country Dance Prior to the 17th Century' *Journal of the English Folk Dance and Song Society*, Vol.VI, No.1 (1949), pp.8–12.

– Some Notes on the English Country Dance Before Playford' *Journal of the English Folk Dance and Song Society*, Vol.III, No.2 (1937), pp.93–99.

Unpublished Works

COOK, TOM 'The Assembly' (1979) – an analytical index of dance and tune forms in *The Dancing Master*, including Volumes 2 and 3 and other country dance books up to 1730. There is a copy in the Vaughan Williams Memorial Library, Cecil Sharp House, London.

HOLMAN, PETER 'A Critical Study and Partial Transcription of *The Theater of Music'* – includes a study of the Playford family and its publications, M.Mus dissertation, King's College, University of London (1971).

MARTIN, JENNIFER KAYE LOWE 'The English Dancing Master, 1660–1728' – a study of the profession of the dancing master in England, Ph.D. thesis, University of Michigan (1977).

MUNSTEDT, PETER 'John Playford, Music Publisher: A Bibliographical Catalogue' – includes all known extant music publications of John Playford (84 catalogue entries) and a compilation of 25 possible lost music publications. Secondary sources relating to Playford's music publications are updated, Ph.D. thesis, University of Kentucky (1983).

NELSON, CLAIR RUSSELL 'John Playford and the English Amateur Musician', Ph.D. thesis, University of Iowa (1966).

Chart of libraries containing copies
of *The Dancing Master*

This chart is based on information in the *Dean-Smith Facsimile* (see p.11), and on details kindly supplied by Margaret Dean-Smith and Peter Munstedt (see p. 12) of other copies which have come to light more recently, or have been lost since the publication of the *Dean-Smith Facsimile*.

The eighteen editions, together with Part II, first and second editions (9A and 9B), are numbered along the top and bottom of the chart. The *Dean-Smith Facsimile* gives details of various imperfections and also of some privately owned copies not included here.

	1	2	3	4	5	6	7	8	9	9A	9B	10	11	12	13	14	15	16	17	18
GERMANY, DDR — Leipzig, Musik Bibliothek der Stadt							•													
GREAT BRITAIN — Cambridge, Rowe Music Library, King's College												•								
Cambridge, University Library																		•	•	
Chichester, West Sussex County Archive Repository			•																	
Dundee, Public Libraries, Wighton Collection				•			•						•	•	•			•		
Edinburgh, National Library of Scotland															•			•		
Glasgow, Euing Music Library (in the University Library)			•																	•
Glasgow, Mitchell Library		•					•				•		•					•	•	
London, British Library, Reference Division	•	•	•	•	•	•	•	••	•		•	•	•	•			•	•	•	•
London, Inner Temple Library				•																
London, London Library																		•		
London, Vaughan Williams Memorial Library, Cecil Sharp House	•		•			•	•	•	•		•	•		•	•	•		•	•	•
Oxford, Bodleian Library		•	•											•				•	•	
Oxford, Bodleian Library, W. N. H. Harding Collection			•		•		•	•										•	•	
Perth, Sandeman Music Library								•	•											
Sidmouth, Sidmouth Museum								•												
IRELAND — Dublin, National Library and Museum of Ireland													•	•				•	•	
UNITED STATES OF AMERICA — Austin, University of Texas																				•
Boston, Public Library, Music Department															•					
Buffalo, Buffalo and Erie County Library															•					
Cambridge, Harvard University Music Libraries																		•		
Los Angeles, University of California, William Andrews Clark Memorial Library											•	•								
Northampton (Massachusetts), Forbes Library					•															
San Marino (California), Henry E. Huntington Library and Art Gallery	•	•																		
Washington, DC, Library of Congress, Music Division											•	•								
	1	2	3	4	5	6	7	8	9	9A	9B	10	11	12	13	14	15	16	17	18

The English Dancing Master:

OR,

Plaine and eafie Rules for the Dancing of Country Dances, with the Tune to each Dance.

LONDON,

Printed by *Thomas Harper*, and are to be fold by *John Playford*, at his Shop in the Inner Temple neere the Church doore. 1 6 5 1.

1   First edition, 1651, title page (see p.5).
See cover illustration for new title page engraving used for the seventh edition, 1686.

2   Eighteenth edition, undated (c.1728); title page engraving used for this edition only (see p.8).

To the Ingenious Reader.

THE Art of Dancing called by the Ancient Greeks *Orcheſtice*, and *Orcheſtis*, is a commendable and rare Quality fit for yong Gentlemen, if opportunely and civilly uſed. And *Plato*, that Famous Philoſopher thought it meet, that yong Ingenious Children be taught to dance. It is a quality that has been formerly honoured in the Courts of Princes, when performed by the moſt Noble *Heroes* of the Times! The Gentlemen of the Innes of Court, whoſe ſweet and ayry Activity has crowned their Grand Solemnities with Admiration to all Spectators. This Art has been Anciently handled by *Athenæus, Julius Pollux, Cælius Rhodiginus*, and others, and much commend it to be Excellent for Recreation, after more ſerious Studies, making the body active and ſtrong, gracefull in deportment, and a quality very much beſeeming a Gentleman. Yet all this ſhould not have been an Incitement to me for Publication of this Worke (knowing theſe Times and the Nature of it do not agree,)But that there was a falſe and ſurrepticious Copy at the Printing Preſſe, which if it had been publiſhed, would have been a diſparagement to the quality and the Profeſſors thereof, and a hinderance to the Learner : Therefore for prevention of all which, having an Excellent Copy by me, and the aſſiſtance of a knowing Friend; I have ventured to put forth this enſuing Worke to the view, and gentle cenſure of all ingenious Gentlemen lovers of this Quallity ; not doubting but their goodnes will pardon what may be amiſſe, and accept of the honeſt Intention of him that is a faithfull honourer of your Virtues, and

Your ſervant to command,

J. P.

3   First edition, 1651, Preface.

(67)

Cuckolds all a row   *For foure*

Meet all forwards and backe ⁛ That againe ⁛

Turne back to back to the Co. We. faces againe, goe about the Co. We. not turning your faces ⁛ Turne back to back to your owne, faces againe, goe about your owne not turning faces ⁛

Sides all with your owne ⁛ Sides with the Co. ⁛

Men change places We. change places, hands all, goe round ⁛ We. change places, men change places, hands all and goe round, to your places ⁛

Armes all with your own ⁛ Arms with the Co. ⁛

Men put the Co. We. back by both hands, fall even on the Co. ſide. men caſt off to the right hand, your We. following, come to the ſame place again ⁛ put them back again, fall on your owne ſide, men caſt off to the left hand, and come to your places, the We. following ⁛

K 2

4   First edition, 1651, 'Cuckolds all a row', showing the layout of the tune and dance instructions used throughout *The Dancing Master* (see p.5).

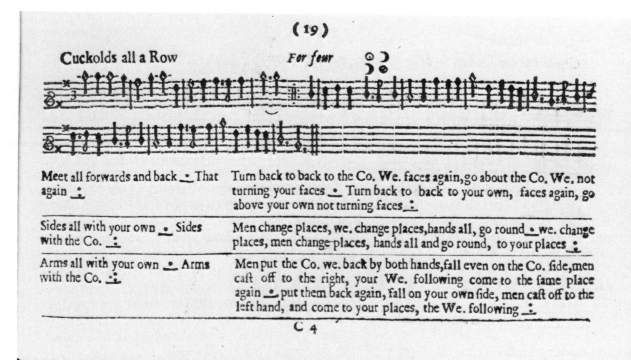

Cuckolds all a Row   *For four*

Meet all forwards and back ⋅ That again ⋮

Turn back to back to the Co. We. faces again, go about the Co. We. not turning your faces ⋅ Turn back to back to your own, faces again, go above your own not turning faces ⋮

Sides all with your own ⋅ Sides with the Co. ⋮

Men change places, we. change places, hands all, go round ⋅ we. change places, men change places, hands all and go round, to your places ⋮

Arms all with your own ⋅ Arms with the Co. ⋮

Men put the Co. we. back by both hands, fall even on the Co. side, men cast off to the right, your We. following come to the same place again ⋅ put them back again, fall on your own side, men cast off to the left hand, and come to your places, the We. following ⋮

C 4

5   Third edition, 2nd printing, 1665 (see p.5).

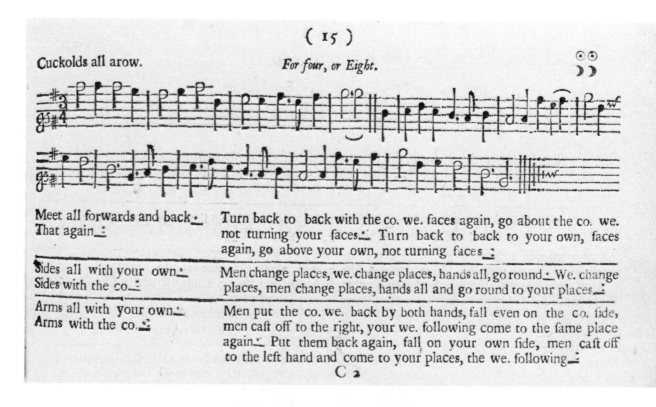

Cuckolds all arow.   *For four, or Eight.*

Meet all forwards and back ⋅ That again ⋮

Turn back to back with the co. we. faces again, go about the co. we. not turning your faces ⋮ Turn back to back to your own, faces again, go above your own, not turning faces ⋮

Sides all with your own ⋮ Sides with the co ⋮

Men change places, we. change places, hands all, go round ⋅ We. change places, men change places, hands all and go round to your places ⋮

Arms all with your own ⋮ Arms with the co ⋮

Men put the co. we. back by both hands, fall even on the co. side, men cast off to the right, your we. following come to the same place again ⋮ Put them back again, fall on your own side, men cast off to the left hand and come to your places, the we. following ⋮

C 2

6   Eleventh edition, 1701 (see p.7).

16

Tunes in the 1st edition, 1651 (1)

1 Adson's Saraband

2 A la mode de France [see no. 71]

3 All in a garden green

4 Argiers *or* The wedding night

5 Aye me *or* The Symphony

6 The Bath [see no. 252]

7 The beggar boy

8 Blue cap (for me)

9 Boatman

10 Bobbing Joe

11 Broom, broom, the bonny, bonny broom

12 Cast a bell

2, separate entry

13 Cheerily and merrily *or* Mr. Webb's Fancy

14 Chestnut *or* Dove's vagary

15 The chirping of the lark

19

16 Chirping of the nightingale

17 Confess(his tune) *or* The court lady

18 The country coll *or* Sir Nicholas Culley

19 Cuckolds all a row

20 Daphne *or* The shepherdess

*In index only of 1

21 Dissembling love *or* The lost heart

22 Drive the cold winter away

23 Dull Sir John

24 Faine I would (if I could) *or* Parthenia [see no. 188]

25 The fine companion

26 The friar and the nun

27 Gathering peascods

28 The glory of the west

29 (The) Goddesses

30 Gray's Inn Mask *or* Mad Tom

31 Greenwood *or* The huntsman

32 Grimstock

33 The gun *or* The valiant captain

34 Half Hannikin

35 Have at thy coat, old woman

36 The health(s) *or* The merry wassail

37 A health to Betty

38 Heart's ease

39 Hit and miss *or* Hit or miss

40 Hockley in the hole

41 Hyde Park

42 If all the world were paper

*In index only of 1

43 The Irish lady *or* Aniseed water Robin

44 Irish trot

45 Jack a Lent

46 Jack pudding *or* Merry Andrew

47 Jenny pluck pears

48 Jog on, (my honey)

49 Kemp's Jig

50 Kettle drum

51 Lady lie near me

52 Lady Spellor (Spillers)

* In index only of 1

53 Lavena *or* The passionate lover(s)

54 The London gentlewoman *or* The hemp dresser *or* The London maid

55 Lord of Carnarvan's Jig

56 Lull me beyond thee

57 Madge on a tree *or* Margery Cree

58 Maiden Lane

59 The maid peeped out at (of) the window *or* The friar in the well

60 The merry, merry milkmaids *or* The merry milkmaids in green

61 The milkmaid's bob

62 Millfield

29

63 Millison's Jig

64 Mundesse

65 My Lady Cullen *or* The Lady Cullen

66 New bo-peep *or* Piccadilly

67 Newcastle

68 The New Exchange *or* Durham Stable (see no. 127)

69 New new nothing

70 The night piece *or* The shaking of the sheets

71 Nonesuch [see nos. 2 and 380]

72 An old man is a bed full of bones

73 The old mole

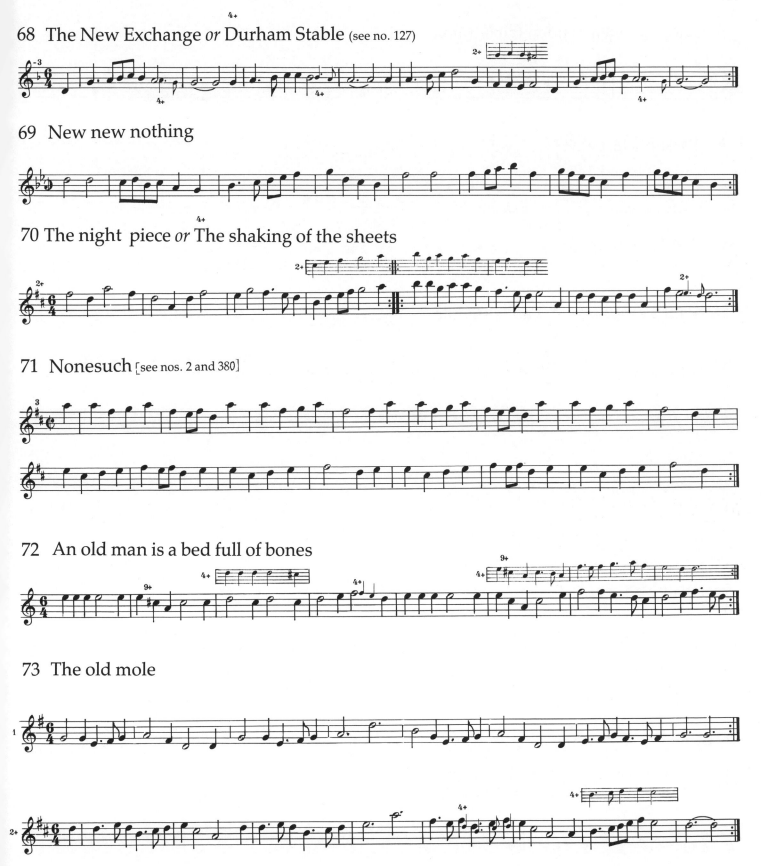

74 Once I loved a maiden fair *or* Maiden fair

75 Parson's farewell

76 Paul's steeple *or* St. Paul's steeple

77 Paul's Wharf

78 Pepper's Black

79 Petticoat wag *or* The tailor's daughter

80 Picking of sticks

81 Prince Rupert's March

82 The Punk's delight (the new way)

83 Rose is white and rose is red

84 Row well, ye mariners

33

85 Rufty tufty

86 St. Martin's

87 The Saraband

88 Saturday night and Sunday morn

89 Scotch cap *or* Edinburgh Castle [see nos. 376 and 533]

90 (The) Sedany *or* Dargason

91 Shepherds' holiday *or* Labour in vain

92 Skellamefago *or* Don Pedro

93 The slip *or* Sir Roger

94 (A) Soldier's life

95 The Spaniard

96 The Spanish gipsy

*In index only of 7+

97 Stanes Morris

98 Step stately

99 Stingo *or* The oil of barley [see no. 303]

100 Tom Tinker

101 Upon a summer's day *or* The garland *or* A summer's day

102 Up tails all

103 The whirligig

104 The wish

105 Woodycock *or* The green man

Tunes new to the 2nd edition, 1652 (2)

106 I love thee once, I love no more *or* Blue breeches *or* I'll love no more

107 Parson(s) upon Dorothy *or* The shepherd's daughter

108 The silver faulken

109 Solomon's Jig *or* Green goose fair

110 Touch and take

111 Trenchmore

112 Under and over

113 Winifred's knot *or* Open the door to three

Tunes new to the 3rd edition, [1657] and 1665 (3)*

114 Abergenny

115 Althea

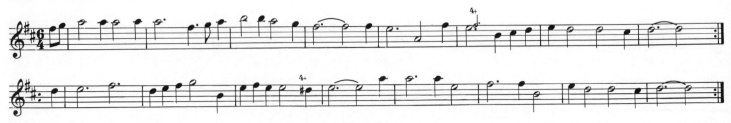

*see p. 4

116 Black nag *or* The galloping nag

117 Chelsea Reach *or* Buckingham House

118 The Devil's dream

119 The Duke of Lorrain's March

120 Gelding of the devil

121 Ginnie pug *or* Strawberries and cream

122 The gossip's frolic

123 Hunsdon House

124 (The) Lady Banbury's Hornpipe

125 Lady in the dark

126 The merry conceit *or* The new conceit *or* The (a)sparagus garden

127 The new New Exchange *or* The new Royal Exchange [see no. 68]

40

128 Oranges and lemons

129 Sellenger's Round *or* The beginning of the world

130 Simple Simon or Huddle-duddle

131 Smith's Rant *or* The cuckoo [see no. 507] *or* May day *or* Smith's new Rant

3A separate entry   6A separate entry

132 Spring Garden

140 A Firk called St. Michell's Mount

141 A frolic [see no. 440]

142 The glory of the north

143 Glory of the sun

144 The haymakers

145 The Highlanders' March [see no. 288]

146 A Hornpipe

147 Iantha [see no. 524]

133 The twins

134 Watton Town's end

135 What you please

Country Dance type tunes from the supplement to the 3rd edition, [1657](3A)

136 An air *or* A Gavotte

137 The ape's dance *or* The Opera

138 Dour's (Dove's) catastrophe *or* Lawyers leave your pleading *or* Love lies a bleeding

139 Dunkirke

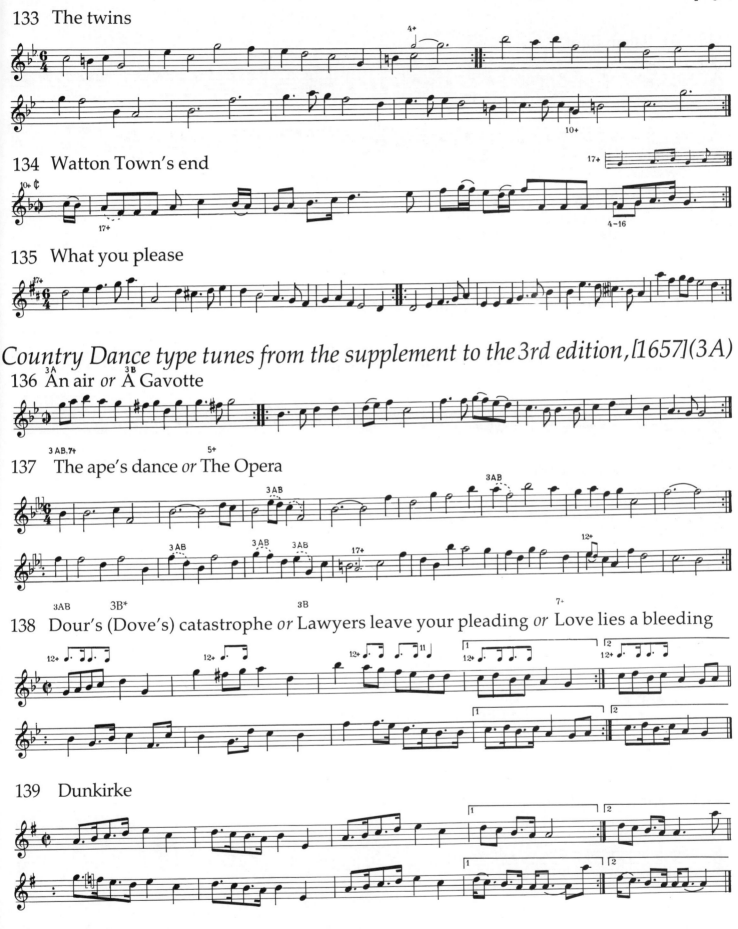

*In index only of 3B

148 An Italian Rant

149 A Jig [see no. 184]

150 The Lady Frances Nevill's delight

151 The Lord Monk's March

152 Mad Dick

153 Mardike

154 A Morisco

155 Moulson's Jig *or* Motson's Jig

156 A new dance *or* Maheney *or* Hey ho my honey [see no. 181]

157 New Rant

158 Porter's dream

159 Porter's lamentation

160 A Scotch Firk

161 Scots Rant

162 Throw the house out of the window

163 The waits

164 Washington's March

Country Dance type tunes from the supplement to the 3rd edition, 1665, (3B), not included in the previous supplement (3A)

165 Amaryllis

166 Antic dance

167 Antic dance

168 Black Jack

169 Bourrée Piccadilly

170 A country dance

171 Coxes dance

172 A dance

173 Duke of York's March

174 A figure dance

175 Freeman's dance

176   The glory of the kitchen

177   A Jig

178   A Jig

179   A Jig

180   The King's delight

181 A new dance [see no. 156]

182 New marrinet

183 New metar

184 The new vagary [see no. 451]

[see no. 149]

185 The old Bourrée

186 Old marrinet *or* Moll Peatly (the new way)

187 On the cold ground

188 Parthenia [see no. 24] or The jovial beggars [see no. 258]

189 The Queen's delight [see no. 527]

190 The running Bourrée

191 The Simeron's dance [see no. 298]

192 Singleton's slip

193 Wallingford House

Tunes new to the 4th edition, 1670 (4)

194 Blue petticoats *or* Green garters

195 Buff coat

196 Catching of fleas

197 Catching of quails

198 Cavylilly man

199   Epping Forest

200   Jamaica

201   The Lady Murray's delight

202   The Lord Chamberlain's delight

203   The maid in the moon *or* **Valentine's day**

204 The mulberry garden [see no. 230] *or* The maid in the mill

205 Northern Nancy

206 Oaken leaves

207 Pegasus *or* The flying horse

208 The phoenix

209 Putney Ferry

210 Put on thy smock on a Monday

211 Sage leaf

212 Sweet Kate

213 Ten pound lass

214 Thomas you cannot

Tunes new to the 5th edition, 1675 (5)

215 Green stockings

216 Newmarket

217 Whitehall

218 The witches *or* Turnham Green

219 The Bourrée *or* Sweet William

220 Bourrée la bass

221 Bouzer Castle

222 Christchurch bells (in Oxon) [a three part round]

223 The cobbler's Jig

224 Dragoon's March [see no. 241]

225 The Duke of York's delight

226 Hedge Lane

227 Hey boys up go we *or* The King's Jig

228 Jack's health

17+ transposed up a tone

229 The King's Jig *or* Winchester wedding

230 The ladies' delight *or* The mulberry garden [see no. 204]

231 The mermaid

232 Nobody's Jig

(232)

233   Old Simon the King

[1st time]

234   Sawney and Jockey *or* Sawney was tall

235 (Mr.) Staggins's Jig

236 Under the greenwood tree *or* Oh! how they frisk it! *or* Leathern apron

237 Well Hall

Tunes new to the 7th edition, 1686 (7)

238 Arcadia

239 Black and grey

240 Country Abigail

241 Dragoon's March [see no. 224]

242 Excuse me

7+   9A+   separate entry

243   The fit's come on me now *or* The Bishop of Chester's Jig

The fit's come on me now

9A+   12+

The Bishop of Chester's Jig *or* The fit's come on me now

244   Greensleeves and pudding pies *or* Greensleeves and yellow lace

17+ Transposed up a tone

245   The Grenadiers' March

246   Haphazard

247 Joan Sanderson *or* The cushion dance

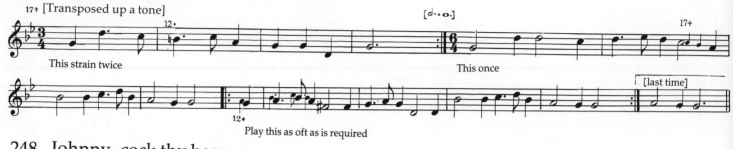

248 Johnny, cock thy beaver

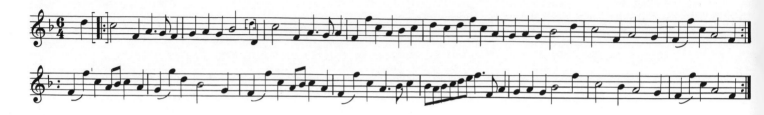

249 The knot

250 Miller's Jig

251 Never love thee more

252 The new Bath [see no. 6]

253 Pall-mall *or* Pell-mell

254 Prince George

255 The rummer

256 Short's Garden(s)

257 Sion House

7A separate entry 9D separate entry

258 The twenty-ninth of May *or* May Hill *or* The jovial crew *or* The jovial beggars [see no. 188]

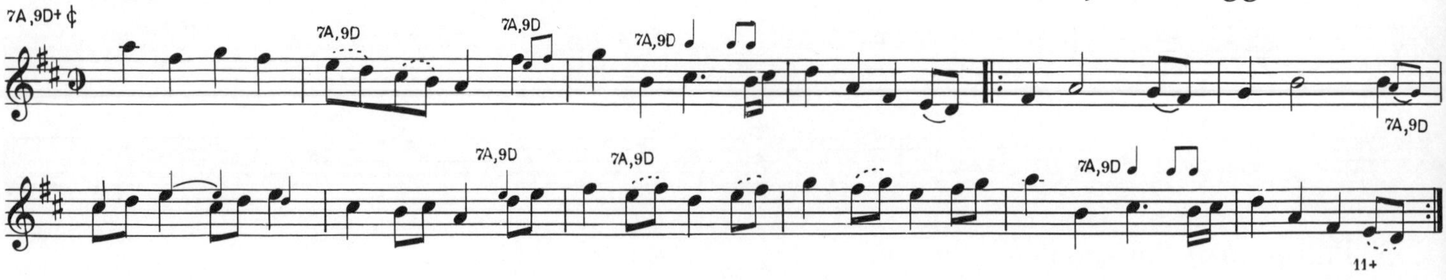

259 Vienna

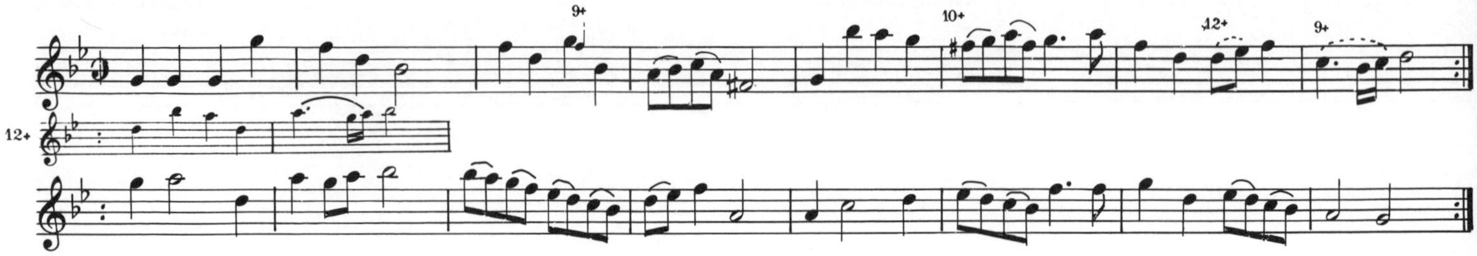

260 Westmorland

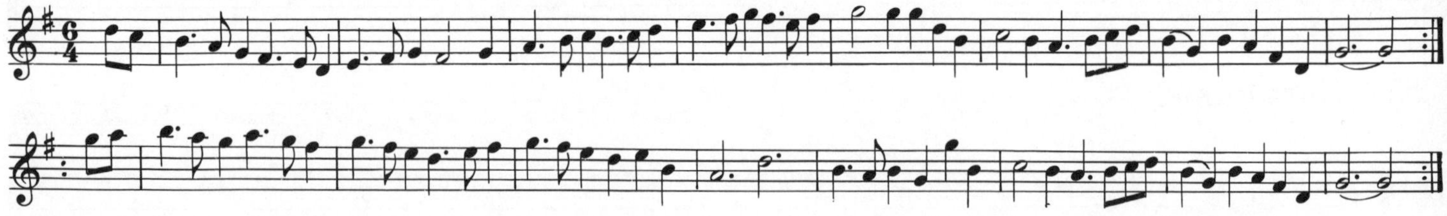

261 Wolverton Hall

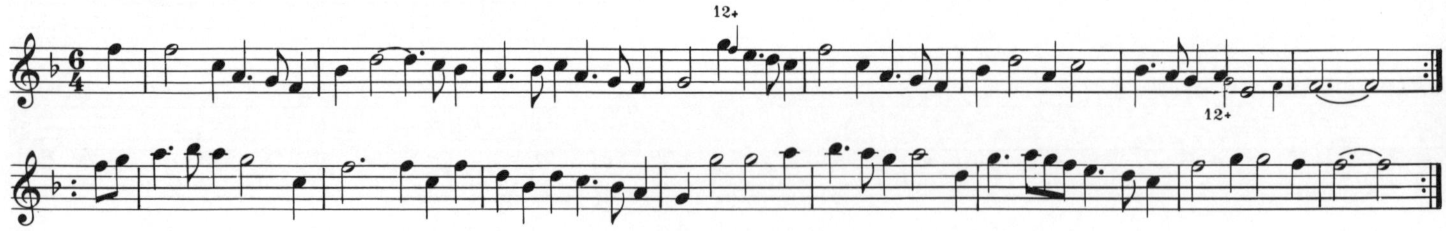

262 Young Jemmy

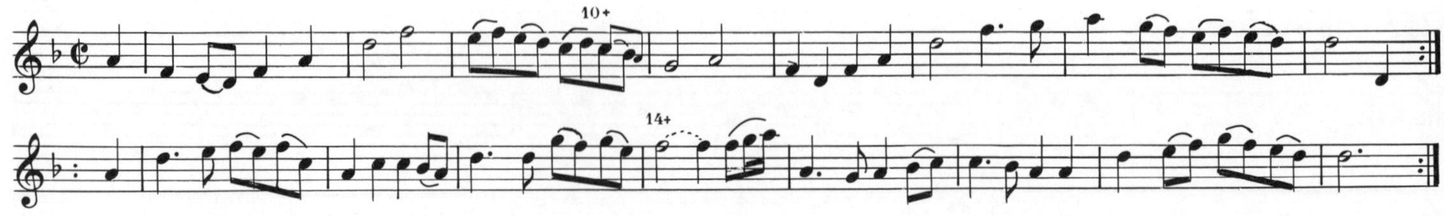

Tunes new to the first supplement to the 7th edition, [1687] (7A)

263 Amboyna

264 Ash Wednesday

265 The blue boar

266 Devonshire House

267 Duke of Grafton's March

268 The green man [see no. 105]

269 Ham House *or* Cherry Garden

270 Hatfield House

271 Hayn's Jig *or* The wanton wife

272 Jenny, come tie my cravat

273 Joan's placket

274 Johnson's Jig

275 The King of Poland

276 Lady Catherine Ogle, a new dance

277 Lady day

278 Mad Robin

279 Michaelmas eve

280 The Miller's daughter

281 Miss Nelly

282 The mug-house

283 New year's eve

Tune the bass string to a 4th[i.e. tune the g string of a violin to a. This means that notes below d' sound a tone higher than written. See also nos. 287 and 442]

284 Prince George's March

285 Richmond Green

286 Round Robin

287 St. Dunstan *or* Clifford's Inn

[This tune only makes sense if the g and d' strings of the violin are tuned up a tone. This means that notes below a' sound a tone higher than written.]

(See also nos. 283 and 442)

288 The Scotchman's dance, in *The northern lass* , *or* The Highlander's March [see no. 145]

289 Sir Foplin

290 Wallom Green

71

Tunes new to the second supplement to the 7th edition, [1688] (7B)

291 Astrope Wells

292 Bonny Dundee

293 Cupid's Garden

294 The Garter *or* King James's March

295 Holyrood day

296 The jockey *or* Four pence half-penny farthing

297 Ladies of London

298 Lady of pleasure [see no. 191]

299 The maid's delight

300 The Mask *or* Hey to the camp

73

301   Painted chamber *or* The country farmer's daughter

Tunes new to the third supplement to the 7th edition,[1689](7C)

302 Bellamira

303 Cold and raw *or* The juice of barley [see no. 99]

304   Maid's Morris

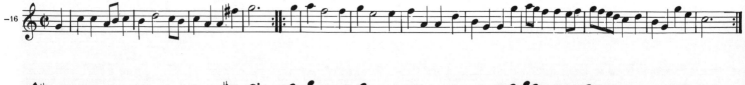

305 Rigaudon *or* The French Rigaudon [see nos. 312, 330 and 450]

306 The siege of Buda

Tunes new to the 8th edition, 1690 (8)

307 Alchurch

308 (The)Emperor of the moon

309 Essex Building(s)

310 I often for my Jenny strove

311 Lilli Burlero

312 A new Rigaudon *or* (The) Old Rigaudon *or* A Rigaudon [see nos. 305, 330 and 450]

313 A Passepied

314 Pool's hole

315 Pretty miss

316 Welcome home, old Rowley

Tunes new to the 9th edition, 1695 (9)

317 Arundel Street

318 Betty's maggot

319 (Mr.) Beveridge's Ground

320 (Mr.) Beveridge's maggot

321 Daniel Cowper

322 Duke of Luxemburgh's March

323 Easter Tuesday

324 Huntington's maggot

325 (Mr.) Isaac's maggot

326 Jacob Hall's Jig

327 Kensington Court

328 (Mr.) Lane's maggot *or* Richmond Ball

329 (Mr.) Lane's Minuet

330 The last new Rigaudon *or* Rigaudon [see nos. 305, 312 and 450]

331   The maid's last wish

17+

332   Marriage hater *or* The intrigues of the town

−13   11+   separate entry

333   The new Bourrée *or* The Indian Queen [see no. 458]

334   Of noble race was Shinkin

335   Old bachelor

336 O mother, Roger

337 Pope Joan

338 Pye Corner

339 Red House

17+ transposed up a tone

340 Rockingham Castle

341 Roger of Coverly

342 Sancho Pancho

343   (The) Siege of Limerick

344   Spanish Jig

345   Tythe pig

346   Valiant Jockey

347   The Whim *or* Bartholomew Fair

348   Whitney's farewell

Tunes new to Part II, 1696 (supplement to the 9th edition) (9A)

349 Black Bess

350 The Britains

351 Bury Fair

352 The Cornish squire

353 (Mr.) Eaglesfield's new Hornpipe

354   Epsom Wells *or* Wa is me, what mun I do!

355   The geud man of Ballangigh; to a new Scotch Jig

356   The happy marriage

357   The happy meeting

358   The happy miller

359 Hobb's wedding: a kissing dance in *The country wake*

360 Irish Bourrée

361 (Mr.) Lane's Trumpet Minuet, to be danc'd with the minuet step

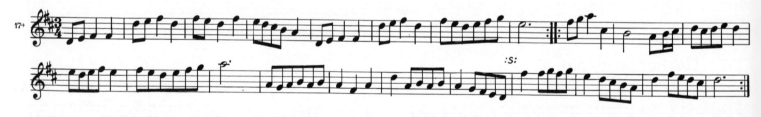

362 Love for love: danc´d in the play

363 Man was for woman made

364 The more the merrier

365 The Purlongs

366 St. Martin's Lane

367 The soldier and the sailor *or* A soldier and a sailor

368 Take not a woman's anger ill, for if one won't, another will

369 'Twas within a furlong of Edinburgh Town

370 (Mr.) Young's delight

Tunes new to Part II, 2nd edition, 1698 (9B)

371 Anna Maria

372 The bonny grey ey'd morn

373 Captain's maggot

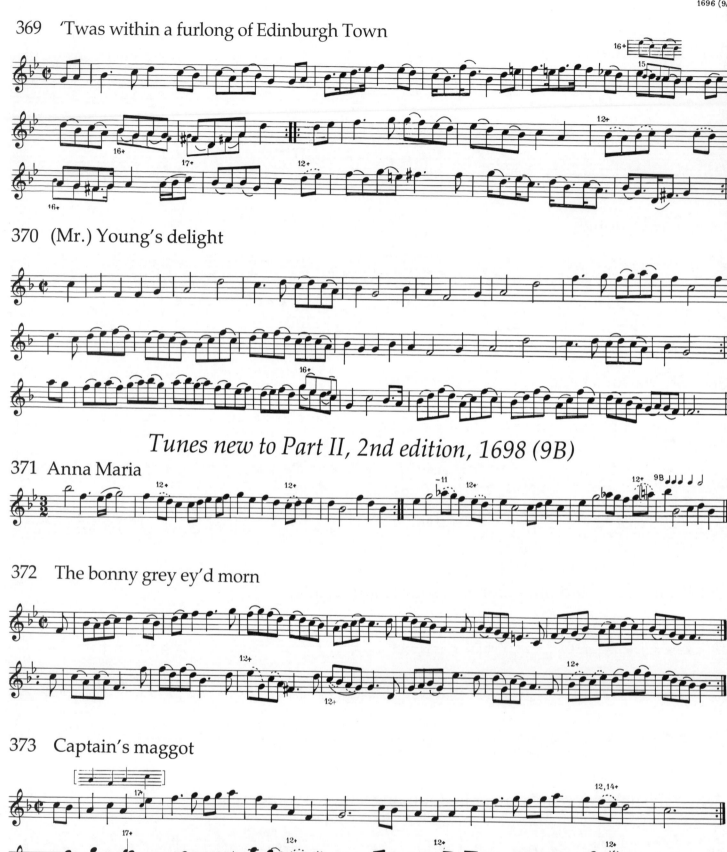

374 De'il take the wars

375 Dunmore Kate

376 Edinburgh Castle *or* The trip to the Jubilee, as 'tis danc'd at the play-house

[see nos. 89 and 533]

377 The hole in the wall

378 Lambeth Wells

379 The Lord Mayor's delight

380 None such (see no. 71)

381 Young Sir Solomon

Tunes new to additional pages in Part II, [1698] (9C)

382 The barley-mow

383 Europe's revels

384 Greenwich Park

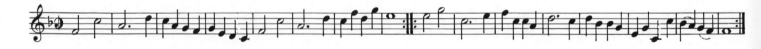

385 Mad Moll

386 The mock match

387 My Lord Byron's delight

388 The sham doctor

389 Shore's trumpet tune

Da capo [al fine]

390 (The)Temple Change

391 Waltham Abbey

392 Westminster Hall

Tunes new to the supplement to Part II, 2nd edition, [1698] (9D)

393 Damme *or* Damey

394 Dr. Pope's Jig *or* The Pope's Jig

395 The Duchess

396 From Aberdeen

397 The Jack's farewell

398 A new Spanish Entrée, and Saraband danced by Monsieur L'Abbé before His Majesty at Kensington, and at the theatre in Little Lincoln's Inn Fields, with great applause

Saraband

399 The sailor's delight [see no. 521]

400 Windsor Castle

Tunes new to the 10th edition, 1698 (10)

401 The coronation day

402 The Dumps

403 Ely Minster

404 Lincoln *or* Bolton

405 The mock hobby horse

406 Puddings and pies

407 The red bull

408 Scotland

409 Three sheep skins

410 Winchester

Tunes new to the 11th edition, 1701 (11)

411 Akeroyde's pad

412 America

[Dal 𝄋 al fine]

413 Barham Down

414 The beautiful Scrabmagg, by G.B.

415 The beaux's delight

416 The Bishop of Bangor's Jig

417 Blackheath

418 Black Nell

12–13 separate entry

419 Buford's March *or* The private wedding *or* Jockey was a dowdy lad

Jockey was a dowdy lad

420 Buskin

421 (The) Carpenter's maggot

[continues with 2nd half as below]

422 Cary's maggot

423 The Catch Club

424 Cheshire Alley

425 Cheshire Rounds

426 Childgrove

427 The cobbler's Hornpipe

428 Cockleshells

429 Crosby Square

430 Czar of Muscovy

431 Dainty Davy

432 The Duke of Gloucester's March

433 Easter eve

434 Ely Court

435 Enfield Common

436 The English Passepied

437 The fiddler's Morris

438 The French ambassador

12+ separate entry   14+

439 Friday night *or* Nowill Hills *or* Love neglected

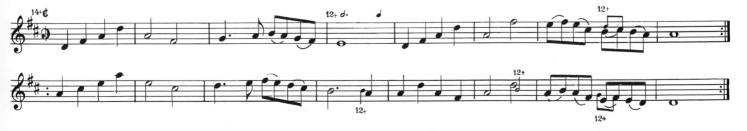

440 The frolic [see no. 141]

441 George's maggot

442 The Gilford

14+ Set up the biggest string one note higher [i.e. tune the g string of a violin to a. This means that notes below d' sound a tone higher than written.

See also nos. 283 and 287]

443 Golden Square

444 The Hare's maggot

445 Hill's maggot

446 The Irish Ground

[from the dance instructions:] The Bass played twice over to every couple when they begin

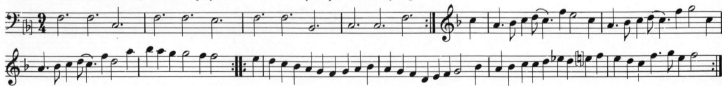

447 The jolly breeze

17+ transposed up a **fourth**

448 The ladies' conveniency

449 The ladies' maggot

450 The last new French Rigaudon [see nos.305 , 312 and 330]

451 The last new vagaries [see no. 184]

452 The Lord Phoppington *or* The new Lord Phoppington [see no. 462]

453 Lumps of pudding

454 The Mansell

17+transposed up a tone

455 Mother Brown's cat

456 Mount Hills

457 My Lord Byron's maggot

458 The new Bourrée [see no. 333]

459 The new Invention

460 New Whitehall

461 Nottingham Castle

462 The pilgrim *or* The Lord Phoppington [see no. 452]

463 Portsmouth

464 The Princess

465 The punch bowl

466 The Queen's Jig

467 Reeve's maggot

468 The Round

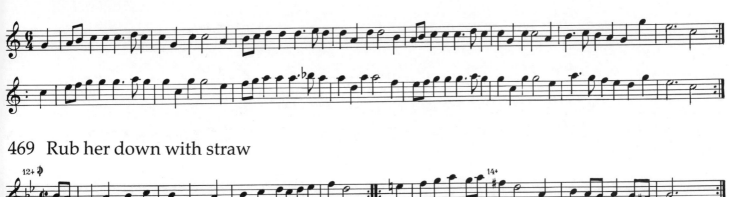

469 Rub her down with straw

470 St. Albans

471 St. Catherine

472 Taylor's trip

473 The Temple

474 The tiger

475 Touch and go

476 Well's humour

477 Whitehall Minuet

478 Wimbleton House

479 Woolly and Georgey

Tunes new to the supplement to the 11th edition, 1702 (11A)

480 Apley House

481 Cottey House

482 The country farmer

483 Dick's maggot

484 Fiddler's maggot

485 Granny's delight

486 Hang sorrow

487 Jack's maggot

488 The jolly boy

489 The ladies' misfortune

490 The man tiger

491 My Lady Foster's delight

492 News from Tripoly

493 Old Abigail's delight

494 Old Noll's Jig

495 Ormond House

496 The Princess's court

497 The Queen's head

498 Slaughterhouse

499   The sword dance

500   A trip to Bury

501   Twelfth eve

502   The Virgin Queen

503   Whely House

Tunes new to the 12th edition, 1703 (12)

504   Bloomsbury Market

505 Christmas cheer

506 The colonel's health

507 The cuckoo [see no. 131]

508 The Devonshire lass *or* Scotch air

509 Fy, nay, prithee John

510 Lincoln's Inn

511 Mayfair *or* Grief a la mode

512 The new Round O *or* Round O

[fine]

[da capo al fine]

513 Nobe's maggot

514 The Queen's birthday

515 The Royal Navy

516 Tunbridge Walks

517 Up with Aily

518 Vigo

519 Wooden shoes

Tunes new to the 13th edition, 1706 (13)

520 Barker's maggot

521 Count Tallard [see no. 399]

522 Draper's Gardens

523 Draper's maggot

524 Iantha [see no. 147]

525 London's loyalty

526 The Marlborough

527 The Queen's delight [see no. 189] *or* The rake's delight

528 (The) Resolution *or* The Quaker's grace

529 The Russel

Tunes new to the 14th edition, 1709 (14)

530 The French King's mistake

531 Hunt the squirrel

532 A trip to St. John's Court

Tunes new to the 17th edition, 1721 (17)

533 Edinburgh Castle [see nos. 89 and 376] *or* Mother Dobney's trencher

534 The gun fleet

535 The Serag's Hornpipe

Commentary

Example

i	ii	iii	iv	v	vi
24.	(1–8).	g₁.	C.	3/wn.	1/10/3/a'. 4/11/1/b'.

Interpretation

i   **24.**   Tune number in this edition.

ii   (1–8).   Editions of *The Dancing Master* which contain the tune, given in brackets.[1]

iii   g₁.   Treble clef on lowest stave line in the first edition (see p.5); applies only to tunes introduced in the first edition.

iv   C.   The original time signature, or that from the earliest edition to include one, followed if necessary by alterations to the time signature which do not form part of the overall changes between editions mentioned on pp.5–8 and ending with the first time signature which accords with the practice of the edition in question (see tune no. **19** for example).

v   3/wn.   The edition in which black notation bn is changed to white wn.

vi   1/10/3/a'. etc   Misprints, irregularities and ambiguities. Edition(s)/bar number(s)/note number(s)/note(s) in Helmholtz notation are given, so this example means: in the first edition, tenth bar, the third note was printed as

---

[1] The following diagram shows how each edition or supplement became incorporated (duly amended) into later editions or supplements. So, when a tune or alteration is given as being found in 9A–18, this means that it was included in supplements 9A, 9B and editions 11-18. Several tunes from the supplements without dance instructions (3A, 3B, 7A) reappear with dances in later editions; in such cases the reappearance is always identified, e.g. a tune included in supplement 7A and editions 9–18 is shown as 7A, 9–18 and not 7A–18.

Editions: 1→ 2→ 3→ 4→ 5→ 6→ 7→ 8→ 9→ 10→11→12→13→14→15→16→17→18

Supplements: 3A   6A⸍7A ⬈   9A   ⬈11A⬈

                                3B   7B⸍   9B⬈

                                      7C⸍   9C⸍

                                            9D⸍

1. (1–8). g₁. 𝄴 .3/wn. 2/4/ ♩ ♪♩ ♩ ♩ ♩ .1–2/5/

♪♪♪♪♪ .   **2.** (1–18). g₁. 𝄵 .2/8/ ♩♩ ♩
.8–16/10/3/c″.   **3.** (1–8). 𝄵 .3+/no key sig.
1/11/ ♪♪♪♩ ♩ .2/15/ ♩. ♪♩ ♪♩ .3+/15/ ♩. ♪♩ ♫
.3+/17/3/sharp.   **4.** (1–8) .g₁. 𝄵 .3/12/2 and 4/c″.
4+/11–12/omitted.   **5.** (1–8) .g₁. 𝄵 .1–2/7/2/f′.
3/2,11/changes occur in 2nd printing (1665) of 3rd ed..
6. (1–8). 𝄵 .1/no upbeat .2/upbeat e″. 3/upbeat g″.
2/7/2/e″.   **7.** (1–8) .g₁. 𝄴 .3/wn.   **8.** (1–8) .g₁. 𝄴 .3/wn.
9. (1–10). 𝄴 .2/no time sig.4/𝄴3.1–10/bn.8+/13/4/f′.
2-3/14/omitted.   **10.** (1–18). 𝄴.1–10/bn.
7/4–5/double bar omitted.   **11.** (1–12) .g₁. 𝄵
.**12.** (1–18). 𝄵.1/2/1/g″.   **13.** (1–18). 𝄴 .11/wn.
1–2/6/4/b′. 4/6–7/bar line omitted.   **14.** (1–8) .g₁. 𝄵
.1/5/5/c‴. 1/8/2/b″. 1/10/6/omitted. 2/11/4 and
1/12/2/f″. 4–5/11–12/ ♩ ♩ ♩ ♩ ♩. ♪|o ‖.
The alternative endings are attempts to correct the 1st
ed., which lacks only the f″ in bar 10 to make sense.
15. (1–8). 𝄴.2/ 𝄵   **16.** (1–8) .g₁. 𝄴.4–5/no time sig..
6/3 .3/wn. 1/8/3/c″.   **17.** (1–10) .g₁. 𝄴   **18.** (1–8) .g₁.
𝄴 .3/wn.   **19.** (1–18) .g₁. 𝄴 .11/¾. 12/⁶₄. 3/wn.
20. (1–8).𝄴.3/wn.   **21.** (1–8). 1,3–4/no time sig. .2/ 𝄴.
5/3 .3/wn. 3/13/1/c″.   **22.** (1–18). 𝄴.11/wn.
3/15–16/d′. 4–6/15–16/no tie. 17–18/18/2/b′.
3/23–24/wn.   **23.** (1–18) .g₁. 𝄴.3(second printing)
no time sig. .4/   3. 3/wn. 1/4,8,12/no ties.
3(1st printing)/11/4/g′. 2/14/2/c″. The other melodic
variants occur in the 2nd printing of the 3rd edition.
24. (1–8). g₁. 𝄴.3/wn. 1/10/3/a′. 4/11/1/b′.   **25.** (1–8).

g₁. 𝄴.3/wn. 3/5/4/omitted thus: ♪♪♪♪
Successive editions make incorrect attempts to
rectify the omission: 4/5 ♪♪♪ .5/5–8/

.
7/5/as 5/5 but note 2/f″ and slur omitted.   **26.** (1–18).
1/ 𝄸.2/ 𝄷.2/10/2/ ♩ .15/14/4/b′ in addition to
printed d″.   15/15/3/c″ in addition to printed e″.
27. (1–8).𝄵.1/18/4/ ♩   .**28.** (1–7,10–18). g₁. 𝄵.
3/3 .4/ 𝄵.   **29.** (1–18). 𝄵. Changes in 3rd edition all
occur in 2nd printing (1665).   **30.** (1–10). g₁. 𝄵, 𝄷,
𝄴, 𝄷, 3.3/6 omitted. 1/17 no key sig.. 1+/25–32/bn.
31. (1–8).𝄴.1+/bn.   **32.** (1–8). g₁. 𝄴.2/no time sig..
3/ . 3/wn. 1/4/omitted.   **33.** (1–10). g₁. 𝄴1/two flats

in key sig.. 3/wn 2/13/2/sharp 2/18/ ♩ ♩♩ .
34. (1–8). 𝄴 .3/8/3 and 3/12/3/sharp. 3/10/omitted.
35. (1–18). 𝄵.3/3–4/ ♪♪♪ .

36. (1–8). 𝄵.**37.** (1–18) 𝄴.4/wn 17+/6/6/d′.
38. (1–8). 𝄴.1+/bn. 1+/4/1/omitted, leading to
incorrect bar lines on the half bar in the second strain
in editions 3–4. 3–4/8/3/omitted. 1–8/12/1/omitted.
39. (1–18). 𝄴.11/¾ barred as ⁶₄. 12/⁶₄. 3/wn.
1/4/1–3/f″d″b′. 2/4/2/a′. 2/4/6/ ♩ .3/6/ ♩· ♩ ♩ .2/8/tie
omitted. 10–11/8/e″. 12+/8/natural. 2/9/4/f′.   **40.**
(1–10). 𝄴 . 3/2/wn, remainder bn.   **41.** (1–3). g₁. 𝄴.
3/wn.   **42.** (1–10). 𝄴.10/ 𝄵3 .1+/bn. 3/2/1/a′.
1/2/2/ ♩· . 1/2/3/omitted. 2–8/6/3/c′. 10/6/3/ ♩· .
43. (1–8). 𝄴 2/ 𝄵.3/3 .1+/bn.   **44.** (1–18). 𝄵.
12/1/2/f″. 1/4/3/ ♩·.12/5/6/c″. 2–11/7/6/e″. 2–11/8/3/d″.
45. (1–8). g₁. 𝄵.   **46.** (1–8). 𝄴.3/wn. 6–7/8/ ♩ ♩· ♩ .
47. (1–8). 𝄴 . 5+/no time sig. for second part. 1+/bn
in first part, wn in second part. 2/7/ ♩· ♪♩ ♩ ♪♩ .
3/7/ ♩· ♪♩ ♩· ♪. 4–6/7/6/natural. 1–2/8/ ♩· ♩ .
3–8/8/ ♩ ♩ . 3–8/9–10/omitted.   **48.** (1–10). g₁. 𝄴.
3/wn   .1/4/1/ ♩ . 3–8/4 contains nine beats
9–10/4/contains 6 beats; remainder rebarred
accordingly. 3/5/8/c″.   **49.** (1–18). 𝄴 .11/wn. 3/4/2/e″.
4–11/11/2/b′.   **50.** (1–8). g₁. 𝄵.
51. (1–8). g₁ 𝄴.1+/bn. 3/3-4/bar line omitted.
52. (1–8). 𝄴.3/ 𝄵.4/3 . 1+/bn. 1/13/4 and 1/14/1
repeated. The 3rd edition version of the tune occurs
in the 2nd printing (1665) only.   **53.** (1–7). 𝄴.3/wn.
1/8/1/ ♩   .**54.** (1–18). 𝄴 .11/wn. 2–3/7/2–3 omitted.
3/8/bar line comes between notes 1 and 2.
55. (1–18). g₁. 𝄵   .**56.** (1–8). g₁. 𝄴.3/wn.   **57.** (1–18).
𝄴 .12/⁶₄ and barred as such. 13/3i barred as ¾. 3/wn.
2–8,12/6/2 no flat.   **58.** (1–10). 𝄵. 1/2/sharp
misplaced to next note.   **59.** (1–8). 𝄴 .3/wn.
60. (1–18). g₁. 𝄴.1/b flat in key sig.. 11+/3i barred
as ⁶₄. 1/3/5 no flat. 1/6/4/g′.   **61.** (1–10). g₁ 𝄴.3/wn.
62. (1–10). 𝄴.3/wn. 5–6/no time sig. .7/𝄴9 .10/ 𝄵3 .
63. (1–8). 𝄴.3/wn.   **64.** (1–7). 𝄵   .**65.** (1–18). 𝄵.
66. (1–18). g₁. 𝄴.3/wn. 3/10/4 no sharp. 4/12,13/ties
misplaced. 4–11/14/1/no sharp. 1/15/1/omitted.
1–2/15/4/ ♩ . 1–2/16/tie omitted. 4/16/tie one note
earlier.   **67.** (1–8) 𝄵.   **68.** (1–7). 𝄴.7/wn. 1/2,4,8/ties
omitted.   **69.** (1–8). g₁. 𝄷1/7/5/omitted.   **70.** (1–8).
g₁. 𝄴.3/wn. 1/5–8/written out three times.   **71.** (1–3).

g₁. ₵. **72.** (1–18). ℭ .3/wn. 1–3/whole tune written out twice, with double bar after bar 8.
73. (1–7). ℭ.2/2/3 ♩· and note 4 omitted. 3(1st printing)/2/4/rest. **74.** (1–10). 1/ ⊕ .2/ ₵.

75. (1–8). g₁. ₵.1/4/2nd time/ 𝄆♩·♩♩𝄇 . 4+/6/omitted. **76.** (1–10). 𝄂.2/13/3/a'.
77. (1–3). ℭ.3/wn. **78.** (1–8). g₁. ℭ .1+/bn. 1–2/7/1/ ♩ .1–7/8/3/d" crotchet. **79.** (1–10). g₁. ℭ .3/wn. 3–9/3/1 has nine beats, taking half of following bar with a tie between b' and b'. Remainder of first strain wrongly barred as a result. 3/11/5 change occurs in 2nd printing (1665).
80. (1–10). ℭ .4/wn. **81.** (1,4–18). g₁. ₵.1/upbeat f'. 1/6/2/ ♩ . **82.** (1–18). 𝄂.4+/note values halved, barring as 12+. 10–11/2/1/a'. 2/9/3/e'. 3/10/1 and 2 reversed. **83.** (1–8). ℭ.1+/bn. 3/1/2,3/g'g'. 1/2 ♩ ♩♩ ♪·♩ . **84.** (1–18). ℭ.6/wn. **85.** (1 only). ₵. **86.** (1–7). ₵. 3/upbeat/d". 3/9/2/d". 5–7/14/2,3/c"d" . **87.** (1–7). g₁. ℭ . 3/wn. The tune sounds better in D minor; there is a version in this mode in Elizabeth Roger's Virginal Book (1656). 2+/the repeats (bars 4–8,13–16) are not written out, but there is a double bar after bar 4.
88. (1–18). ℭ.6/wn. 1/1,3/4/g". 7/3/2/d".
89. (1–10). ℭ.3/wn. 3/10/ ♩ ♩♩ ♩ . Perhaps this tune should be in the major mode. Otherwise bars 9 and 11 need altering with either a b' flat or f' sharp; alternatively change the b's in these bars to c".
90. (1–8). ℭ . 3/wn 2+/alternative titles reversed.
91. (1–10). 3–7/**3** . 8–9/ ℭ**3** . 10/ ₵**3** .3/wn. 1/12 to end/ 𝄆♩♩♩♩♩♩♩♩ 𝅗𝅥 𝅗𝅥𝄇 .
92. (1–8). ℭ.3/wn. **93.** (1–18). g₁. ₵.2/4 and 2/12/ ♫ ♩ . **94.** (1–18). g₁. ℭ . 3/wn. 10/7/4/omitted. 12/7/2–3/omitted. **95.** (1–3). g₁. 2/ ₵. The three bar phrases of this tune do not fit the dance instructions. There is a version in ⁶₄ with two bar phrases in Elizabeth Roger's Virginal Book (1656), so perhaps the tune should be rebarred as suggested.
96. (1–18). ℭ.3/wn. 2/upbeat/f". 3+/upbeat/d". 10/1/6/omitted. 2/3/ ♩♩♩♩♩ ♩ .2–3/8–9/no 𝄐 . 13/12/between 2–3/f" ♩ . **97.** (1–3). 1/time sig. unclear. 2/ ₵ . **98.** (1–10). ℭ.3/wn. 1/4/1/a'.
99. (1–8). ℭ .6/wn. **100.** (1–10). g₁. ℭ. 3/wn. 1/5/1/omitted. 6–7/6/3/a'. 1/7/4/ .7/7/7/e".
101. (1–8). g₁. ℭ . 3/wn. 2–3/9/3/d". **102.** (1–8). 𝄂.
103. (1–7). g₁. ℭ.3/wn.
104. (1–8). ℭ . 3/wn. 1/3/4/ ♩ . **105.** (1–8). ℭ . 3/wn.
106. (2–8). ℭ.3/**3** .4/𝄡 .5–6/**3** .7+/𝄡 .3/wn. 3/10/1/d". 4/10/between 4–5/bar line.
107. (2–8,6A–18). ₵. 'Parson upon Dorothy' is

retitled 'The shepherd's daughter' in 4–8. The title 'Parsons upon Dorothy' then re-enters separately in 6A with a slightly different tune. 'The shepherd's daughter' drops out after 8. 9–13/1/4/sharp. **108.** (2 only). ℭ.f sharp key sig.. 2/8/4/ambiguous, could be d'. **109.** (2–10). ℭ.3/wn. 10/14/2/b'. **110.** (2–3). ℭ. 2+/bn. **111.** (2–18). ℭ .6/wn. 3/4/6/b'. 12/8/3/a'.
112. (2–18). ℭ.3/wn. **113.** (2–16). 2/ ℭ .3/**3** barred as ⁶₄. 8/ℭ**3** . 11/⁶₄. 12/⁹₄ and correct barring. 11/wn.
114. (3–18). 𝄂.3/4/ 𝄆♩♩·♩♩𝄇 . **115.** (3–7) **3** .
116. (3–18). **3** .9–11 c sharp from key sig. omitted.
117. (3–8). **3** .3/11/2nd half of bar omitted; rest of tune wrongly barred as a result. 3/16/1/ ♩ .
118. (3–18). **3** . 6+/5 and 6/sharp omitted, so play b flat in bar 6. 4/7/after 5/additional bar line.
119. (3–18). ₵.3/double bar omitted. **120.** (3–8). ₵. 3+/bn. **121.** (3–7). **3** . **122.** (3–18). **3** .
123. (3–18). **3** . **124.** (3–8) 3+/ ₵ and barred accordingly. 3–6/4/1/a". **125.** (3–8). **3** . **126.** (3–7). **3** . 3/8/4/ ♩ . 4+/11/5/sharp. **127.** (3–18). ₵.5–8/2/5/g".
128. (3–8). ₵.4/ ℭ**3** . 4–5/1,3/slurs under notes 2–3.
129. (3–8). 3–4/ ℭ**3** . 5+/ ℭ**5** . 4+/15/1/sharp.
130. (3–10). 𝄂. **131.** (3–18,3A,6A). 𝄂. 3/double bar omitted. 6A,9+/have different dance instructions.
132. (3–18). **3** . **133.** (3–13). **3** . **134.** (3–18). 𝄂. 18/3/1/g". 18/3/6–7/f"g". 17+/4/5/ ♩ . **135.** (3–18). 6/**3** . **136.** (3AB). 𝄂. 3B/9/6–7/ ♩· ♪· .
137. (3AB,5–18). **3** . 12/13/3/a". **138.** (3AB,7–18). ₵. 17+/4(2nd time) and 8(1st time)/7/omitted.
139. (3A). ₵. **140.** (3A). 𝄂. **141.** (3A). **3** .
142. (3AB). 𝄂. **143.** (3AB). 𝄂. **144.** (3A). **3** .
145. (3AB). **3** . **146.** (3A). **3** . 2nd half possibly lacks 1½ bars between bars 7 and 8. Bars 9 and 10 would then be rebarred as in 1st half. **147.** (3A). ₵.
148. (3AB) 𝄂. **149.** (3A). **3** . **150.** (3AB). ₵.
151. (3AB). 𝄂. 2nd half wrongly barred because of short bar 8. **152.** (3A). **3** . **153.** (3AB). **3** .
154. (3AB). ℭ**3** . 3B/8/3–4/ ♩· ♪ .
155. (3AB,4–10). **3** . **156.** (3AB, 7–18). **3** .
157. (3AB). **3** . 3B/2/3/e'. **158.** (3AB). **3** .
159. (3AB). **3** . 3A/key sig. on g' stave.
160. (3AB). **3** .3B/3/3/g'. **161.** (3AB). **3** . Perhaps bar 3 should be omitted to make a 4 bar phrase.
162. (3A). **3** . **163.** (3AB). **3** . 3B/4/6/omitted
164. (3AB). **3** . 3AB/15,20/extra bar line half way through each bar. 3B/19/1 and 2/reversed.
165. (3B,4–18). ₵. **166.** (3B). 𝄂. Syncopated bars notated: ♩ ♩♩ ♩ . **167.** (3B). **3** .
168. (3B,4–18). **3** . 3B/4/3/omitted. **169.** (3B). ₵.
170. (3B). **3** . **171.** (3B). **3** . 3B/10–12/ 𝄆♩♩♩♩♩ 𝅗𝅥 ♩ 𝅗𝅥 𝅝𝄇 .

172. (3B).**3** . **173.** (3B).**𝄼** . **174.** (3B) No time sig.. 3B/3/ 𝅗𝅥 ♩♩♩♩ . 3B/8/ 𝅗𝅥· 𝅗𝅥 𝄇 . 3B/14/ 𝅗𝅥· 𝅘𝅥 𝅘𝅥 . **175.** (3B).**3** . 3B/11/ ♩♩♩♩ 𝅗𝅥 ♩ . **176.** (3B). **𝄵** . **177.** (3B). **𝄼** . **178.** (3B).**3** . **179.** (3B).**3** . 3B/6/3/could be a′. **180.** (3B).**3** . **181.** (3B).**3** . 3B/11/4/leger line missing. **182.** (3B). **𝄼** . **183.** (3B).**𝄵** . **184.** (3B,4–7,9D–18).**𝄵** . 12–13/1/2/c′. 12–13/1/4/d″. **185.** (3B). **𝄵** . **186.** (3B,4–18).**3** . 11+/new dance instructions. 4–11/7+/

. **187.** (3B).**3** . **188.** (3B,11–18).**3** . **189.** (3B).**3** . **190.** (3B). **𝄵** . **191.** (3B).**3** . 3B/9/only 3 beats. In Musick's Handmaid (Pt.1), 1663, the melody in bars 9–10 goes:

. (see also no.298). **192.** (3B,4–18). **𝄼** . **193.** (3B,4–18).**3** . **194.** (4–10).**C3** . **195.** (4–18). **𝄵** . 13,17+/3/1/c″. The first version may be a mistaken attempt to force a ⁶₄ melody into **𝄵** . **196.** (4–10).**C3** . 9+/3/1/e″. **197.** (4–10).**C3** .**198.** (4–18). **𝄵** . see no.195. **199.** (4–8).**C3** . **200.** (4–18). **𝄵** . 12/7/3,4/d″c″. **201.** (4–8).**C3** . 5+/8/1/b′. **202.** (4–8). **C3** . **203.** (4–8,6A–18). **C3** . **204.** (4–18). **C3** . **205.** (4–18). **C3** . **206.** (4–8).**C3** . **207.** (4–7).**𝄵3** . The three bar phrase (bars 9–11) seems unlikely. One solution is to repeat bar 10. Another solution is to play bar 11 before bar 10 as well as after it. **208.** (4–10). **𝄵** . **209.** (4–8).**𝄵3** . **210.** (4–8).**C3** . **211.** (4–18). **C3** . 4/ **C3** . 5–7/ **𝄵3** . 11/⁶₄. 12/ **3** . for bars 1–2, ⁶₄ bar 3. 13+/⁶₄ throughout. 4–11,13–16/no key sig.; f always sharpened apart from 1st bar, except 4–8/10/3/natural. 12/f sharp key sig., f natural 1st bar. 17+/1/3/not naturalised. **212.** (4–18). **𝄵3** . **213.** (4–18). **𝄵** . **214.** (4–7). **C3** . In 7 title is 'Paul's Steeple'; correct version of 'Paul's Steeple' (no.76) is elsewhere in 7. **215.** (5–18).**C3** . 10/5/5/omitted. 7–8/7/4/c″. **216.** (5–18). **𝄵,C3** . 12–13/26 end/double bar. 17+/2/1/c″. 17+/25/1,2/e″d″. 18/26/4/f″. **217.** (5–18). **C3** . 6/4/2/c″. **218.** (5–18). **𝄵3** . 10–12/1/2/f″. 14+13/5/e″. 12/15/4/b′. **219.** (6A–10). **𝄵** .6A/10/3/e″ **220.** (6A–18). **𝄵** . **221.** (6A–18). **C3** . 16/7/2/b′. 17/8/3/e″ in new key. 18/8/3/f′ in new key. 12/10/2–4/d″d″c″. **222.** (6A–18). **𝄼** . 17+/15/4/c″. **223.** (6A–18).**𝄵** . Bar 10 as suggested by Chappell to correct 7 bar phrase (PM, p.278). **224.** (6A,9–18). **𝄵** .

6A/8+/

. In 7–8 this title has a completely different tune (no.241). **225.** (6A–18). **C3** . 18/7/1/a′. **226.** (6A–18). **𝄵** . 12/1/8/e′. 16+/7/5/b′ sharp. 13+14/no repeat sign. **227.** (6A–18). **𝄵** . 9/8/2/omitted. See no.195. **228.** (6A–18). **C3** . 17+9/2/a″ in new key. **229.** 'The King's Jig':(6A–13) 6A–11/ **𝄵** and barred as such. 12/⁹₄. 13/ **𝄵** .'Winchester wedding':(9B–18) 9B–11/no time sig., barred as **𝄵** . 12+/⁹₈. 16+/2/1/e′. 12/5/2/e″. **230.** (6A–8,7A).**C3** . **231.** (6A–18).**C3** . **232.** (6A–18). **𝄵** .7–8/15–16/ crotchets. **233.** (6A–18).**C3** . 7/4/1/e″. 6A/9/7/omitted. 6A–10/16/3/g″. **234.** (6–18). **𝄵** . **235.** (6A–18).**C3** . 6A/4/6/f″. 9–11/10/4/no natural. 7–8/11/3/c″. **236.** (6A–18). **𝄵** .7A/ **C3** . 9/⁶₄. 17+/3/1/d″. 9+/4/𝅘𝅥· 𝅘𝅥· . **237.** (6A–18). **C3** . 7–9/**C3** . 10/³₂. 7–9/15/ ♩ ♩ ♩ ♫ ♩ . 7–11/15/5/f″. 17+/15/5/𝅗𝅥 . **238.** (7–18). **𝄼** . **239.** (7–18). **𝄵** . 13+/7/6/c″. **240.** (7–18). **C3** . 18/5/2/c″. 18/9/6/g″. 9–11/14/3/g″. 7–8/15/5 to bar 16/4 omitted. **241.** (7–8). **𝄵** . This tune replaces no.224. **242.** (7–18).**3** . 17+/19/3/natural omitted. 12–13/20/1–2 slurred. 17+/20/1/a′. **243.** (7–18).**C3** . The two versions exist separately in 11–13, but are merged under the joint title in 14+ with the music from 'The fit's come on me now'. 9A+/8/2/in 'The Bishop of Chester's Jig' only. The slurs in 12+ occur in 12–13 in 'The fit's come on me now' only. **244.** (7–18).**3** .**245.** (7–18). **𝄵** . 13+/4/2/a′. 13+/4/ 𝅘𝅥· ♫𝅘𝅥· ♫ . 18/16/3/omitted. **246.** (7–18). **𝄵** . **247.** (7–18). **C3** . 7–11/5/⁶₄ omitted, and remainder barred as ³₄. **248.** (7–18). **C3** . **249.** (7–18). **𝄵** . **250.** (7–18). . 7/ **C3** barred as ⁶₄. 10/ **𝄵3** . 11/⁶₄. 12/⁹₄ and correct barring. 7+/6/8–9 slurred, instead of notes 7–8. **251.** (7–18).**3** . **252.** (7–18). **C3** . 18/8/tie omitted. **253.** (7–18). **𝄼** . 18/11/6/e″. 7–9/12/3/e′. 10/12/3/omitted. **254.** (7–18). 7–9/ **C3** . 10/ **𝄵** . 12/7/3/omitted. **255.** (7–18). **C3** . **256.** (7–18). **C3** . 11,13+/6/1/f″. 7/10/ties omitted. **257.** (7–18). 7–10/ **C3** . 11/⁶₄. 12/³₂. **258.** (7–18,7A,9D). **𝄼** . The 7A version of the tune appears in 9D with the title 'The Jovial Beggars'. However, in 11+ this title has a completely different tune (no.188), but the same dance instructions as 9D. **259.** (7–18). **𝄼** . 9–11/10/2–3/e″f″. 9–11/10/4/a″. **260.** (7–18).**3** . 7–9/15/2/f′. **261.** (7–18). **C3** . 15–16/6/1/c″. **262.** (7–18). **𝄵** . **263.** (7A). **𝄵** . **264.** (7A). **C3** . **265.** (7A).**3** . 'The Blew-Bore'. 'Bore' was an English spelling for Bourrée (see p.00) but in this case the pub name seems more likely, as Bourrées are never in ⁶₄. **266.** (7A,10–18). **C3** . **267.** (7A). **𝄵** .

268. (7A). **C3** . 269. (7A). **C3** . 270. (7A). **3** .
271. (7A). **C3** . 272. (7A,7B–18). 7A/ **C3** barred as $\frac{6}{4}$. 7B/ **C3** barred as $\frac{3}{4}$. 10/ **¢3** . 11/**3i**. 12/$\frac{6}{4}$ and barred as such. 273. (7A,10–18). **C3** . 7A,9–11/c sharp in key sig.. 7A/1/1/dot omitted. 7A/9–10/omitted. 10/12/no tie. 274. (7A,9–18). **C3**.
275. (7A,10–18). 7A/ **C3** barred as $\frac{6}{4}$. 10–11/no time sig., barred as $\frac{3}{4}$. 12/**3** . 13/**3i** . 14/$\frac{6}{4}$ and barred as such. 10–16/no e flat in key sig.. 7A–13/second

strain: [music notation] *etc.*
10+/5/5/natural omitted. 276. (7A). **D**.
277. (7A,10–18). **D**.11/1/bar line omitted. 15+/1/5/a'.
15/3/1–2/ [music] . 10–11/6/1/b'. 14–17/8–9 bar line omitted. 278. (7A,9–18). **¢**. 9–10/11/1/no sharp.
279. (7A). **C3** . 7A/14/3/d". 280. (7A). **C3** .
281. (7A). **C3** . 282. (7A,10–18). **C3** .
283. (7A,10–18). **3** . 7A/4/1/c'. 10–11/8/2/a'. 11/8/3/g'.
284. (7A). **¢** . 7A/10/6/a'. The 2nd half is unsatisfactory. The slur over the double bar probably indicates a first and second time bar [music 1. 2.] [music] and thus a wrongly barred 2nd half. Even so, the last 4 bars still fail to make musical sense. 285. (7A).**C3** . 286. (7A). **3** . 7A/8/2/e".
287. (7A). **¢**. 288. (7A,9B–18). **¢**. 289. (7A). **C3** .
7A/3/4/sharp. 290. (7A). **C3** . 291. (7B–18).
7B–9/ **C3** barred as $\frac{6}{4}$. 10–11/$\frac{6}{4}$. 12/$\frac{9}{4}$ and rebarred. 12-16/double bar omitted. 292. (7B–18). **C3** .
11/4/1/e". 293. (7B–18). **C3** . 7B–10/6/6/e".
11+/8/3/ ♪ . 11/16/bar line omitted.
294. (7B–18). **¢**. 295. (7B–18). **¢**.12–13/7/4/a".
11/7–8/bar line omitted. 296. (7B–18). **C3** .
7B–11/6/4/b'. 17+/7/4/f'. 10/9/3/e". 12–13/12/1/f'.
297. (7B–18). **3** . 298. (7B–18). **C3** . See no.191 for bars 9–10. 7B–8/10/5/g'. 299. (7B–18). **C3** .
300. (7B–16). **C3** . (9C–18). 12+/$\frac{6}{4}$. The two titles have separate entries in 11–16. 301. (7B–18). **C3** .
302. (7C–18). **D**. 18/7/3–4 beam omitted.
303. (7C–18). **3** .(7C–8). **3** .9(both)/ **C3** barred as $\frac{3}{4}$.
10/ **¢E** . 12/$\frac{6}{4}$ and barred as such. 304. (7C–18). **¢** .
305. (7C–18). **¢**. 7C–18/1st strain barred:
| [music] |etc.. 7C–10,12/1,2,3/2–4/ [music]
*to be played [as] Demi-quavers. 306. (7C–18). **¢**.
307. (8–18). **C3** .
308. (8–18). **D**. 16/7/1/f'. 8–12/16/2/sharp.
309. (8–18). **C3** . 13–14/5/1/f". 310. (8–18).
8–9/ **C3** barred as $\frac{3}{4}$. 10/ **¢3** . 11/**3i** . 12/$\frac{6}{4}$ and barred as such. 311. (8–18). **C3** . 9–10/ **¢3** .11/$\frac{3}{4}$ barred as $\frac{6}{4}$. 17+/11/3/c". 312. (8–18). **C3** . 9/ **¢**.
8 appears to be an attempt to make the tune fit $\frac{3}{2}$:

[music notation staves]

313. (8–18). **C3** .12,14+/rebarred: $\frac{3}{2}$ [music] | [music] etc.. 314. (8–18). **¢**. 315. (8–18). **C3** .
8–10/3/ [music] . 12/3/4/omitted.
316. (8–18). **¢**. 317. (9–18). **C3** . 318. (9–18). **C3** .
10–11/9/2/g'. 9–11/10/2/b'. 319. (9–10). **¢**.
320. (9–18). **C3** . 9–10/ **C3** . 11/$\frac{6}{4}$. 12/$\frac{3}{2}$. 321.
(9–18). **¢**.17+/10/3/missing. 322. (9–18). **¢**.
323. (9–18). **C3** . 10/8/2/a'. 9–10/10/6–7/f'e'.
324. (9–18). **¢**. 17+/28/1/e". 325. (9–18). **C3.**
10/ **¢3** . 11/$\frac{3}{4}$. 12/$\frac{3}{2}$. 326. (9–18). **C3** .
15–16/19/ [music] . 17+/19/ [music] .
327. (9–18). **¢**. 9–13/5–6 [music].
9–10/7/4/sharp. 328. (9–18). **¢**. 9–10/2/1/ ♪ .
10–11 also contain a song for the tune, 'Strike up drowsie Guts-Scrapers' by Thomas d'Urfey.
9+/:S: above bars 1 and 9. 329. (9–18). **C3** .
18/8/1/d". 330. (9–18). **¢**. 11+/2/10/e'.
331. (9–18). **DD** .10/ **¢3** . 332. (9–18). **C3** .
11–13/1/ [music] . 333. (9–13). **¢**.
(11–18). 14/ **¢**. 334. (9–18). **¢**. 335. (9–18). **3** .
9–10/7/5/sharp. 336. (9–18). **¢**.18/20/1/d".
337. (9–18). **¢**. 14/3/1/c". 14/4/1/b'. 11/9/3/f".
12/9/3/omitted. 11,13/13/2–3/slur omitted.
9–11/20/4/b'. 338. (9–10). **C3** . 339. (9–18). **¢**.
9–10/1/ [music] .17+/3/1/a' in new key.
12/15/7/c". 340. (9–18). **C3** .9–10/ **C3** barred as $\frac{3}{4}$.
11/ **3i** . 12+/$\frac{6}{4}$ and barred as such. 341. (9–18).
9–11/$\frac{3}{9}$. 12/$\frac{9}{4}$. 342. (9–18).**C3** . 12/1/bar line after rest. 11–12/15/ [music] . 13+/15/ [music] .
343. (9–18). 9–10/**3** . 11/$\frac{6}{4}$. 12/$\frac{3}{2}$. 344. (9–18). **C3** .
345. (9–10). **C3** . In Purcell's King Arthur (1691) as the tune 'Harvest Home', bars 5–10 are omitted, but bars 11–14 are repeated, with a *petite reprise* of the last two bars each time. 346. (9–18). **C3** .
11/4/2–3/slur omitted. 347. (9–18). **C3** .
348. (9–18).**C3** .9–10/2/ [music] . 9–11/6–8/
shortened: [music] .
349. (9A–18). $\frac{6}{4}$. 15/5/no bar line at start.
9B/6/3/omitted. 350. (9A–18).**3** . 16+/5/1/a'.
16/13/4/flat omitted. 351. (9A–18). **¢**. The first 4 strains are printed, and numbered 1–4, with the instructions "Play each strain twice and end with the third strain." 14-16/2/2/f'. 352. (9A–B). **3** . 9B/$\frac{3}{2}$.
353. (9A–18). **3** . 354. (9A–18). **C3** . Up to 12 each title is printed separately with the same tune but different dance instructions. 11/16/variant slur is in

125

'Wa is me', not 'Espom Wells'.   **355.** (9A–18). **3** .
356. (9A–18). **3** .   **357.** (9A–18). **3** .   **358.** (9A–18). ₵.
359. (9A–18). **C3** . 17+/1/5/d″.   **360.** (9A–18). ₵.
17+/2/4–5/no beam. 15+/7/1/e′.   **361.** (9A–18). **C3** .
9A–11/20/**:S:** and not at bar 15.   **362.** (9A–18). ₵ .
363. (9A–18). ₵.13/16/double bar omitted.
364. (9A–18). ₵. 9A–9B/6/4/sharp.   **365.** (9A–18). **3** .
15+/10/2/b′. 16+/12/2/d″. 11+/double bar omitted.
366. (9A–18). ₵.   **367.** (9A–18). **3** . 11,13/2/2/e′.
18/15(end of)/double bar. 18/17(end of)/bar line one
note early. 9A–13/22/2/missing, hence end reads:
| 𝅗𝅥 ♩ ♩. ♪𝅘𝅥 | 𝅗𝅥 ♩ ♩ ‖ .   **368.** (9A–18). **2** .
11/9/1–2/slur omitted. 18/17/1/g′.   **369.** (9A–18). ₵.
17+/13/2nd slur omitted. 11,13+/16/3/sharp omitted.
370. (9A–18). ₵.   **371.** (9B–18). **3** .   **372.** (9B–18). ₵.
11/12/ ♫♫ ♪♩. ♪ . 16+/13/1/f′.   **373.** (9B–18). ₵.
13/10/3/f″. 9B/14/2/f″.   **374.** (9B–18). ₵. 17+/2/3/a′
(at new pitch). 15+/7/1st slur omitted.
375. (9B–18). ₵. Song printed in 9B only, beginning
"There lately was a Maiden fair, with ruddy Cheeks,
and Nut-brown Hair,". 9B/13/2/e″.   **376.** (9B–16,
11–18). 'Edinburgh Castle': 9B/**3** .11/**3i** barred as⁶₄.
12/⁹₄ and rebarred. 'The trip to the Jubilee': 11/⁶₄. 12/⁹₄
and barred as such. The slurs in bars 1–3, 5 and 7
occur in 'Edinburgh Castle', editions 9B–11, and also
in 'The trip to the Jubilee', editions 11–18, though
omitted in bars 1 and 3, editions 9B–13, both titles.
11/12/1–2/a′b′. 11+/"The second strain but once" in
dance instructions.   **377.** (9B–18). **3** . 9B/4/1/a′.
378. (9B–18). ₵. 9B–11/first repeat signs omitted
(printed **:S:** in 12). 11–14/8/double bar omitted.
13–14/16/3–4/slur omitted. 15+/16/5/d″.
379. (9B–18). 12–13/**3** . 14–17/**3i** . 18/**3** .
380. (9B–18). ₵**3** . 9B/4/2/e″. 12–13/13/1st slur
omitted.   **381.** (9B–18). **3** . 12/1/3/omitted.
9B–13/8–12/The words "bass" and "treble" are
omitted.   **382.** (9C–18). ⁶₄. 11+/4/tie becomes a slur
one note earlier. 17+/11/6/d″.   **383.** (9C–18).
9C–11/no time sig., barred as ₵. 12/³₂ and barred as
such. 11/1/1/ ♩ .   **384.** (9C–18). 12/ ♪ . 17+/5/1/a′.
17+/8/1/f″.   **385.** (9C–18). 9C–11/no time sig., barred
as ⁶₄. 12+/⁹₄ and rebarred. 9C–11/1/1/b′.
386. (9C–18). 12/ ♪ . 11/1/3/g′.   **387.** (9C–18). ₵.
18/4/2–3/beam omitted. 18/11/3/d″.   **388.** (9C–18). ³₂.
16/2/2/ ♩ .   **389.** (9C–18). 11/ ₵. 13,15+/7,8/3/b′.
390. (9C–18). 12/⁶₄.   **391.** (9C–18). 12/ ♪ .
12/13 ♩ ♪♩ ♩ ♫ .   **392.** (9C–18). 12/³₂. 13/2/6/d″.
12/7/4/d″. 9C/9/3/d″. 9C/10 ♩ ♪♩. ♩ ♩ ♩ .
393. (9D–18). ₵. 9D/1/3/omitted. 11/2/additional bar
line after note 6.   **394.** (9D–18). ₵ . 13/6/1st slur
omitted.   **395.** (9D–18). ⁶₄. 13/13/6/d″.

396. (9D–18). ♪ 12+/2/4/♩. **397.** (9D–18). **3** .
18/7/3/f″.   **398.** (9D only) ⁶₄, **3** . Appears on last
page without dance instructions. Saraband has **:S:**
over first and last notes.   **399.** (9D–18). ⁶₄.
400. (9D–18). ⁶₄.   **401.** (10–18). ₵.10/9/ | ♫♩ | .
402. (10–18). ⁶₄. 12,14/ +/³₂. 2nd half: 10–11,13/⁶₄ and
barred as such. 12,14+/⁹₄ and rebarred. 10+/last

bars:

. in 13+

the figures 1 and 2 come slightly earlier thus:

. In dance instructions: "The
second Strain played as many times as there is
c[o]uples".   **403.** (10–18). 10/**3** . 11/**3i** .
17+/4/omitted. 17+/12/sharp omitted. 12/17/1/c″.
17+/22/slur omitted.   **404.** (10–18). 12/⁶₄. 10/2/1/g″.
10/4/4–5/g′a′. 11+/4/4–5/b′c′ (these two notes were
probably printed upside down in 10th ed., and then
wrongly corrected in 11th ed.). 12/5/5/a′. 11–12/6/2/b.
13+/6/2/d′.   **405.** (10–18). 12/⁶₄.   **406.** (10–18). 12/⁶₄.
17+/11/5/b′.   **407.** (10–18). 12/⁶₄. 15+/4/ ♩. ♩♩ .
408. (10–18). 10/no time sig., barred as ⁶₄. 11,13/⁶₄.
12,14+/⁹₄ and rebarred.   **409.** (10–18). ₵.
410. (10–18). 12/⁶₄. The omission of the suggested
notes (bar 8) makes the remainder of the tune
wrongly barred.   **411.** (11–18). 12/ ₵. 12/double bar
omitted. 14–16/5/8/e″. 14+/16/1,2/e″.   **412.** (11–18).
12/ ♪ . 17+/"The first strain twice and the second
once and from the repeat. And the Minuet, the first
strain once and the last once, and end with the first
part".   **413.** (11–18). 15/⁶₄.   **414.** (11–18). ⁶₄.
12–13/1/6/g. 11,13/2/2/e″.   **415.** (11–18). ⁶₄.
416. (11–18). 12/⁶₄.   **417.** (11–18). ₵. 18/1/4/f″.
12/19/1/f″.   **418.** (11–18). 12/⁶₄.   **419.** (1–18) and
(12–13). 12/ ₵ in both versions. 'Jockey was . . .' bar
11, has notes 5–6 reversed in 12th ed..   **420.** (11–18).
12/ ♪ .   **421.** (11–18). ⁶₄. 12–13/12/6/g″.
422. (11–18). 12/³₂. 11/1/ ♩. ♩ ♩ . 11–13/8/ ♩ ♩ ♩ ♩ .
17+/12/7–8/slur.   **423.** (11–18). 12/⁶₄.
15+/upbeat/f″.   **424.** (11–18). 12/⁶₄.   **425.** (11–18).
11/³₄. 12/³₂.   **426.** (11–18). ₵. 11/3/omitted.
427. (11–18). 12/³₂.   **428.** (11–18). ₵.   **429.** (11–18).
12/ 13/4/1/c″.   **430.** (11–18). ⁶₄. 11+/key

sig. . 13/6/5/b′. 11+/10,12,18/accidentals
placed one note later. 11+/11/1st accidental placed
one note later. 11–12/12/6/f″. 12/last bar/d″d″.
11+/The figures 1 and 2 indicating 1st and 2nd time
bars are printed one bar later.   **431.** (11–18).
12/ ₵.   **432.** (11–18). ₵. 11/7/3/e″.   **433.** (11–18).
12/ ♪ . 11+/1/2–4/ ♩. ♫ . 13/13/3/e″.   **434.** (11–18).
12/ ♪ . 13+/11/5–6/b′a′.   **435.** (11–18). ³₄. 12/³₂.

436. (11–18). $\frac{3}{4}$. 15/$\frac{3}{3}$. 16+/$\frac{3}{2}$. 437. (11–18). 12/ ¢.
12/15/♩ ♩ ♩. ♩ . 11/16/1/b'. 18/16/2/e'. 438. (11–18).
12/ ¢. 439. 12/ 𝄽. Variants, including time sig.,
are in 'Nowill Hills' only, as is 12/7/7/g'.
440. (11–18). 14/ ¢. 17+/7/2/a'. 17/9/5/g'.
441. (11–18). $\frac{6}{4}$. The unusual phrase structure in the
second half makes an omission seem likely. Since the
tune bears a resemblance to 'Packington's Pound',
the latter's harmonic and phrase structure has been
used for the 1½ bars insertion. 442. (11–18). ¢.
11–13/All b's have a sharp (indicating a transposed c'
sharp for the scordatura). 443. (11–18). 12/$\frac{6}{4}$.
444. (11–18). 11/$\frac{6}{4}$. 12/$\frac{3}{2}$. 12/1/extra bar line after note 1.
12/6/no double bar. 13/9/5/d'. 11+/14/♩ ♩ ♩· .
445. (11–18). 14/ ¢. 12/14/4/omitted. 13+/14/4/d'.
446. (11–18). 12/$\frac{9}{4}$. 11/ground bass written a sixth
lower (i.e. as if for treble clef), apart from bar 2/note
3/B. 18/treble clef for ground bass, but notes remain
in same position on stave. 13/10/6/e'. 447. (11–18).
14/ ¢. 11/3/1–2/♫ . 17+/13/2nd,3rd,5th,6th slurs
omitted. 17+/14/3rd,4th slurs omitted. 17+/17/2/f'.
448. (11–18). 15/$\frac{6}{4}$. 449. (11–18). 12/$\frac{6}{4}$. 11–12/7/5/f'.
11/9/no upbeat. 11/9/1–2/f''g''. 12/9/2/e''.
450. (11–13). 2 . 451. (11–18). 12/$\frac{6}{4}$. 452. (11–18).
12/ ¢. 11/2/1/e''. 17+/4/1/d'' at transposed pitch.
17+/10/1/e'' at tranposed pitch. 17+/14/4/b' at
transposed pitch. 453. (11–18). 12/$\frac{6}{4}$. 454. (11–18).
12/ ¢. 12/9/3/e''. 17+/11/9/a' at transposed pitch.
455. (11–18) 15/ ¢. 17+/3/3/sharp. 17+/8/notes in
reverse order. 17+/23/4th slur omitted. 456. (11–18).
11/2nd half starts with a 3 bar phrase:
etc. 457. (11–18). 12/$\frac{6}{4}$.
11–13/14/2nd rest omitted. 458. (11–18). 13/ ¢.
459. (11–18). 12/$\frac{6}{4}$. 12/4/4/c'. 11+/16/1st and 2nd time,
slur over notes 1–3. 460. (11–18). $\frac{6}{4}$. 11–13/no double
bar. 461. (11–18). 12/$\frac{6}{4}$. 462. (11–18). 12/$\frac{6}{4}$.
15/2/3–4/d''. 11/4/♩ ♩. ♪. 11+/11/1/sharp.
11/11/ ♫♫♩. ♪.11/12/♩ ♩. ♪. 'The Pilgrim' is on an
adjacent page to no.452 'The Lord Phoppington', so
the use of 'The Lord Phoppington' for this tune may
be a mistake. 463. (11–18). ¢. 17/7/5/b'.
464. (11–18). 12/$\frac{6}{4}$. 11–13/16/3/omitted.
465. (11–18). 3i . 12/$\frac{3}{4}$. 15+/9/7/b''. 13–16/12/1/d''.
18/14/1–2/slur. 466. (11–18). $\frac{6}{4}$. 11 omits note 2 and
the dot from note 1 in bars 2,6,10,14, making a variant
with unequal phrase lengths. 467. (11–18). 11/ ¢.
12/$\frac{6}{4}$. 468. (11–18). 12/$\frac{6}{4}$. 469. (11–18). ¢.
470. (11–18). $\frac{6}{4}$. 11/2/3/♩ 471. (11–18). 12/ ¢.
15/20/1/c''. 472. (11–18). 12/ ¢.
473. (11–18). 12/ ¢. 14/9 has a key sig. of two flats
(start of second line; third line reverts to one sharp).

474. (11–18). 11/$\frac{6}{4}$. 12+/$\frac{3}{2}$. 475. (11–18). 12/ ¢.
16/7/1/b'. 476. (11–18). 11/3i . 13/6/5/b'. 12/7/7/e''.
477. (11–18). 12/3 . 17+/12/2/a''. 478. (11–18). 12/ ¢.
11/8/3–4/♩. ♪. Bar 1 could be repeated after bar 3 to
make two 3 bar phrases in the 1st half.
479. (11–18). 3i . 11,13–14/8/1/f'.
480. (11A–18). ¢. 481. (11A–18). 12/$\frac{6}{4}$.
482. (11A–18). 14/ ¢. 483. (11A–18). $\frac{3}{4}$. 12/$\frac{3}{2}$.
484. (11A–18). ¢. 11A/5/1/g''. 12/23/3/d''.
485. (11A–18). ¢. 12+/1/3/a'. 486. (11A–18). ¢.
487. (11A–18). ¢. 11A,13+/15/1/sharp.
488. (11A–18). ¢. 489. (11A–18). $\frac{6}{4}$. 11A+/all
semibreves printed as ♩·♩. 11A/6,8/ties omitted.
490. (11A–18). ¢. 16/2/2/♩ . 12/12/1/f'.
491. (11A–18). 𝄽. 11A–16/11/3/sharp. 18/15/6/sharp
omitted. 492. (11A–18). $\frac{6}{4}$. 12/$\frac{3}{2}$. 13/8/4/d''.
12/9/6/omitted. 11A/11/7/f''. . 493. (11A–18). 12/$\frac{3}{2}$.
11A–15/double bar omitted. 494. (11A–18). $\frac{6}{4}$.
15–16/7/5/g''. 12/14/4/b'. 12/20/2/g' 495. (11A–18). ¢.
496. (11A–18). ¢. 497. (11A–18). $\frac{6}{4}$.
498. (11A–18). $\frac{6}{4}$. 12/12/1/c''. 499. (11A–13). ¢.
12/double bar omitted. 500. (11A–18). ¢.
11A–14/2/♩ ♩. ♫ . 12/3/5/e''. 501. (11A–18). ¢.
502. (11A–18). 12/$\frac{9}{4}$. 503. (11A–18). 15/ ¢.
11A/6/. 12+/6/4–5/semiquavers.
504. (12–18). 14/ ¢. 17+/6/7/e' . 12/double bar
omitted. 12/9/2–3/quavers, note 4/semiquaver.
505. (12–18). 3 . 15/10/3/f'. 14/11/1–3/f''g''f''.
12/18/2–3/g'c''. 506. (12–18). ¢. 15/11/1/g''.
17+/14/5/omitted. 18/15/1/g''. 507. (12–18). ¢.
12/19/4/g'. 508. (12–18). ¢. 509. (12–18). ¢.
12/6/8/a'. 17+/7/3,7–8/e''f'a'. 12/9/7/c''. 17+/10/6/c''.
510. (12–18). 14/ ¢. 511. (12–18). $\frac{6}{4}$.
12–14/10/2/dotted. 512. (12–18). 𝄽. 16/1/6/♩ .
13/32/2/d'. 513. (12–18). $\frac{9}{4}$. 18/1/1/b'.
514. (12–18). 2 . 17+/4/3/e'' at transposed pitch.
515. (12–18). ¢. 516. (12–18). $\frac{6}{4}$. 17+/1/3/ ♩ .
517. (12–18). $\frac{9}{4}$. 518. (12–18). $\frac{6}{4}$. 15/6/4/flat omitted.
519. (12–18). ¢. 520. (13–18). 14/$\frac{3}{2}$. 13/1/5/omitted.
13/8/6/omitted 14+/10/6/d'. 521. (13–18). $\frac{6}{4}$.
522. (13–18). 3i . 523. (13–18). 14–17/3i . 18/3 .
14+/7/4/g. 524. (13–18). ¢. 525. (13–18). 14/$\frac{4}{4}$.
526. (13–18). 2,3. 527. (13–18). 14/3i . 18/8/3/d''.
14/9/slur omitted. 528. (13–18). 𝄽. 14/8/7/e''.
13/14/2–3/d''c''. 13+/16/3–4/c''d''. 529. (13–18). $\frac{6}{8}$.
530. (14–18). $\frac{6}{4}$. 14/12/tie omitted. 531. (14–18). $\frac{6}{4}$.
532. (14–18). 15/ ¢. 14+/6/6/sharp. 14+/16/3/sharp.
533. (17–18). $\frac{6}{4}$. Replaces no. 376 534. (17–18). ¢. A
version in $\frac{6}{4}$ in Playford's *Apollo's Banquet*, 1690, has b
naturals and e naturals in bars 9–11. 535. (17–18)
17+/no time sig.; barred as $\frac{6}{8}$. 'Serag's' in title and
index but 'e' looks very like 'c', i.e. 'Scrag's'.

Tune index

For this index, all tunes are transposed to C major or minor (accidentals are not shown). The index proceeds alphabetically from the first note of the first bar of each tune. Upbeats are shown, but do not form part of the alphabetical progression. Oblique strokes represent bar lines.

Upbeat/Opening of tune		Tune no.						
G/ABCBAG/ABCAGEG/D	6/4	406	CCCBA/BAGD	6/4	108	AB/CCG/ECAB/CADC/B	C/2	490
ABCBCA/AGEC	6/4	279	CCCBA/BCDED	6/4	16	CCGE/FDBB	6/4	99
G/ABCBC/DDDEF/	6/4	301	CCCBA/BGGEF/GGE	6/4	197	CCGE/GA/GFEDC/DG	6/4	451
G/ABCCB/CEFG/AD/G	6/4	218	ED/CCCB/CCD/EBB	C/2	147	CCGEGE/CCGEFED/CC	9/4	517
G/ABCCCAGEG/D	9/4	341	GAB/CCCBC/DCBAGAB/C	C/2	150	CCGFE/DDABC/BAG	6/4	448
G/ABCC/CBC/EFGG/	3/4	403	CCCB/CEDCDB/C	3/2	383	CCGF/GABBB/CCGE/CE	6/4	303
G/ABCCCDC/CGCCA/BCD	6/4	468	E/CCCBC/GCCBC/DGE/	C/2	95	C/CCGG/EDECDC/DEDG	6/4	180
G/ABCCDCCG/ABC	9/4	233	CCCC/BAGA/BCBFGE/D	6/4	242	CD/BABCC/D	6/4	118
G/AGAB/CC	6/4	42	CCCC/BGE/BGCE	C/2	259	G/CDBCG/CDEDD/EBG	6/4	441
C/BABC/DE/FGFEDE/DCC	6/4	84	CCCCC/CC/DEFED/E	C/2	119	CDB/CGE/DEC/DCBAG/	3/4	329
E/BAGF/EDCE	C/2	431	CCCC/CCCE/DCBA/G	/2	222	CDCBAG/AAGFE/FGEGG	6/4	323
C/BCDE/DCDBG	6/4	111	CCCC/CC/DDBC/D	C/2	26	G/CDCBAG/AG	6/4	335
G/BCG/ABGFE/FDGE/DC	C/2	295	CCCC/DCBG/ACAG	6/4	89	CDCBAGFED/CDEF	9/8	535
C/BGAB/CCC/BG	C2	232	CCCCDE/DCAG/EDCCDE	6/4	194	G/CDCBCDG/GDEFGEF/	6/4	400
C/BGDD/BAGDG/	6/4	78	CCCCD/EDCG/FEDEFG	C/2	64	G/CDCBCG/AEFD/B	6/4	281
GC/BGDEF/EDC	6/4	398	CCCC/EFE/DBBB/B	/2	76	C/CDCBG/EDG/G	6/4	37
C/BGGAB/CE/BGFD/C	6/4	156	CCCCGE/FGEDC	6/4	206	G/CDCCCG/CDCCCG/CDE	6/4	350
CAAGB/CDEEGG/	6/4	163	AB/CCCDDD/EDEFGGAB/CC	6/4	145	CDCCDC/BCDDCB/C	6/4	49
CACGAB/CAGEG/	6/4	157	G/CCCDE/CCCBA/GGE	6/4	527	G/CDCDCD/EF/G	C/2	116
CAC/GEG/CACD/E	C/2	316	G/CC/CDE/DC/A	3/4	59	G/CDCDEF/EDCG/ABCBA/G	6/4	280
CBD/CAEFD/ECEDB/C	3/2	435	ED/CCCDE/DDDEF/ECEFG	6/4	317	CDCEE/DEDF/EGCFE	6/4	311
AB/CA/GAGEFG/F	6/4	66	CCCDE/DECDBG/E	C/2	142	CDCEFG/BCDEDBG/	9/4	513
CAGFEF/GCG/CBABC/B	C/2	263	CCCCECC/EDEFECC/	6/4	201	CDCEGG/CE/DEDDAC/B	6/4	421
CBAB/CCC	C/2	15	E/CCCE/DDDG/CCCE/CCC	C/2	288	G/CDCGG/CDCGB	6/4	318
CBA/BCDBG	C/2	249	CCCG/AGE	6/4	31	C/CDCGG/EC/CDCBG/A	6/4	60
CBAGE/FAGFEDC	C/2	330	G/CCDB/ECFD/G	6/4	46	G/CDEBG/FGEBG/CDEC/G	6/4	204
G/CBA/GEG/AGF/EDG	3/4	398	CCDCG/CE/DDEDA/DF	C/2	322	CDECA/GABCD	6/4	39
CBAGFE/FDDD	6/4	98	G/CCDDEFGE/FEDCC	C/2	184	CDE/CBCB/AGC/CBC	6/4	407
C/CBA/GFE/FEDC/GFE	C/2	358	CCDE/CC/FFAGE/DD	3/4	159	CDECDBG/ABCEDC	6/4	300
C/CBAGFE/FGED	6/4	193	G/CCDEC/DGG/EDCDCB/C	C/2	432	G/CDECDE/FGABCBA/	6/4	129
CBA/GG/AAB/C	C/2	312	CCDEC/GEABCBG/C	3/2	493	G/CDECE/FEEFG/EFE	6/4	466
CBCBA/GFEEGE/DEFGABC	C/2	393	CCDEC/GGG	C/2	30	CDEDG/DEFBE/ACBDCDE/G	3/2	343
CBCDBABG/AGADG	C/2	226	CCDEDC/AABCCGE/	3/4	465	CDECGEC/EFGEAG/	3/2	492
G/CBCDC/CBCDC/DG/G	3/4	338	CCDEDC/BADG/	C/2	234	G/CDECGF/EFGEAA/	6/4	315
G/CBCDCDCD/EDEFEFEF/G	C/2	507	CCDEDC/CGABCG	C/2	374	C/CDEDBG/CDEE/FGAG	6/4	345
G/CBCDEDC/EFGGA/GAGE	C/2	372	CCDEDC/FDDEFED/EDC	3/4	479	G/CDEDCB/AA/GEFEDC/D	C/2	463
CBCD/EDEFDB/	6/4	23	G/CCDEDC/EDGG/AGFE	/2	484	G/CDEDC/BABGE/	6/4	215
G/CBCDEF/ECEF/GAGBC/D	6/4	293	CCD/EDE/FFED/C	C/2	85	G/CDEDC/BAGGA/BBBAG	6/4	424
CBCDEFGEG/ECEDDG/	6/4	269	CCDEEF/GGGEF/GGAGF/E	C/2	284	G/CDEDCB/CAG	6/4	171
CB/CE/DCCDC/B	6/4	24	G/CCDEFD/EFE	C/2	107	C/CDEDC/BCDG	6/4	38
CBCG/ABCBG/	6/4	32	CCDEF/EDCBG/	6/4	47	CDEDC/BCGC/CBC	C/2	136
CBCGCEDG/BDFDECGE	C/2	411	CCDEF/GCG/AAGF/GGFE	3/4	523	G/CDEDCB/CGEFG/	6/4	152
G/CBCG/CGG/AFEDG/EC	C/2	401	G/CCDE/FGEDC/FFDG/	C/2	336	CDEDC/GAGC/BAGAB/G	6/4	189
CBCG/ECGF/EDCG/BC	6/4	133	B/CCDEF/GGABC/DEFG	6/4	423	CDEDCG/BCDCB	C/2	44
CBCG/EDCBG/CGFGFE	/2	433	CCDEF/GGGF/EEFGFED/	C/2	245	CDEDCG/CGGFGB	C/2	140
CBCGE/FGAGEC/B	6/4	404	G/CCEC/ECDE/FBBF/	/2	253	G/CDEDC/GED/EFGDC	6/4	187
CBC/GFEDEFEC/CDE	3/2	320	CCEDC/BGBB/CCEDC	6/4	105	C/CDEDC/GFED/EFG	6/4	141
G/CCABC/BDCB/CAAF/G	C/2	304	CCEDC/DDF	C/2	29	AB/CDEDEC/BABC	6/4	215
C/CCABC/DBG	6/4	73	GEG/CCEDC/DGEG/CCEDC	3/2	154	G/CDEDEC/BCDGC/BAG	6/4	416
CCBA/ABCE/EFGG	C/2	198	ED/CCEEF/GEEAG/F	/2	173	G/CDEDEC/BGCE	6/4	122
C/CCBAB/CCG	6/4	53	CCEE/FGFC/	6/4	132	CDEDEC/CBGE	6/4	279
CCBAG/AGFED/EDCB	6/4	199	G/CCEFEDG/CC	9/4	113	CDEDECDCBAG	6/4	300
CCBAGB/FDBBC	3/2	520	CCEF/GABBB/CC	/2	114	CDE/DEF/BB/B	3/4	43
CCBA/GE/DBAG/FGFGFED/C	C/2	339	G/CCEFG/GABD/DEF	C/2	362	CDEDE/FEDCBG/AFDG/ED	C/2	391
CCBAGFE/DEF/GFED	3/2	264	AB/CCEF/GGBC/DEF	6/4	298	G/CDEDEF/EEF/GABAG/G	C/2	86
CCBA/GF/EFG	6/4	112	AB/CCEF/GGBC/DFEG/DC	6/4	191	CDEDG/ABCBAG/C	6/4	289
C/CCBA/GFEFG/FEDC	C/2	227	CB/CCEG/AG/ABCABCDC/BAG	/2	386	G/CDEDG/CCCCG/C	C/2	267
CCBC/AG/AABG/CG	C/2	223	CCEG/AGABCD/EFG	C/2	487	G/CDEDG/EDCBAG/C	C/2	254
CCBC/DCBAGA/FFEF/	C/2	183	GAB/CCEG/AGFGB/EDCBAGFE	C/2	412	CDEE/CDEC/EDCE/DCBAG	3/4	361
CCBC/DEFD/EFG	6/4	205	AB/CCEG/CDAB/CCEG/CC	C/2	499	G/CDEEDE/CDDDCD/EDC	6/4	467
G/CCBCG/FEDC/B	6/4	299	CCFD/ECF/DBB	C/2	239	B/CDEED/EGABC/D	6/4	218
CCBCGFE/DEFEDCB/	3/2	525	G/CCGCCE/DCA	6/4	8	C/CDE/EFG/GAG/DEF/	3/4	342
CCBG/CD/EEDB/E	6/4	33	AB/CCGC/FDAB/CCGC/EC	C/2	437			

Code	Meter	No.
CDEFC/FGAGF/GABC	6/4	110
CDEFDC/BGG	C/2	4
G/CDEFDE/DCB	6/4	332
CDEFDG/FGEGFEDCB	6/4	410
G/CDEF/ECC/BGAGEF/D	6/4	429
ED/CDEF/ECD/EFG	C/2	469
G/CDEFE/DCBAG/	6/4	153
G/CDEFEDC/BCDG	C/2	440
CD/EFED/CDDC/DGEG	C/2	473
G/CDEFED/EDCGE/F	6/4	297
G/CDEFED/G	6/4	68
C/CDEF/GABB/CDCBA/G	6/4	175
G/CDEFGA/BCDEFE/DG	6/4	217
ED/CDEF/GABG/CDED	C/2	185
G/CDEF/GA/GFEDE/FE	6/4	188
G/CDEF/GB/AGABC/G	6/4	121
G/CDEF/GB/CDEDC/BG	6/4	209
C/CDEF/GCC/BABC/D	6/4	348
CDEFGC/CBCDG/	C/2	138
C/CDEFG/CD/EFGAB/E	6/4	125
CDEFGE/FEDCDG	C/2	139
CDEF/GE/FGFEFD/GD/	C/2	409
G/CDEF/GFEDFG/AGFE	/2	192
CDEFGG/AGFGG	C/2	148
CDEFG/GCBCD/	6/4	135
C/CD/EF/G/GC/BG/AF/G	3/4	21
CDEF/GGGG/AG	6/4	17
CDEG/CBA/CBA	C/2	508
E/CDEG/EAGEDC/EDD	C/2	428
C/CDG/CED/CFEDG/C	6/4	137
CDGEDC/DCAG/	C/2	128
CEAGCE/DBF/	3/4	237
G/CEC/BGB/CEC/BG/CEC	3/4	505
CECCG/BCDEDC	6/4	25
C/CECD/BAGCB/	6/4	355
C/CECDFAB/CBAG	6/4	100
CEC/GADEFF/E	C/2	506
CECGE/AFDFGA/C	C/2	488
CE/DBAB/CGED/EC	C/2	195
CEDBG/ACBGE/F	C/2	509
CEDBG/CEA/GECBCDG	6/4	511
CEDC/CEDC/CEDC	6/4	402
CEDC/GE/BFDB/FEDCB	C/2	319
CED/ECDEFEDC/CEE/DCBA	3/2	422
CE/DE/FEDCDCBA/G	C/2	363
CEECE/BDDBD/CEECE	6/4	296
CEEFG/AGA/GEE	C/2	200
G/CEFEDC/BDG/CEFF	C/2	246
G/CEF/GEAFDG/EC	6/4	481
CEF/GE/FD/GD/	C/2	409
CEFGE/FGEFDC/	C/2	131
C/CEF/GFEDCC/DEFD	C/2	510
CE/BAGAB/CDE	6/4	186
CEG/CDCG/CDCG/	C/2	508
CEGC/GE/FGAGFE/D	/2	439
CEG/DEDCBD/G	3/2	392
CEGG/CGFEDE/FGE	C/2	454
CFFG/AGFGG/	/2	182
CB/CGACB/CCDCB/CG	/2	528
CGAE/FDFEDC	6/4	172
CGAGEC/AGAD	6/4	162
CGA/GE/CDEDC/CDEDC	6/4	531
CGA/GFEDDEFFG/AF	3/2	371
CGAGFE/FGAGFEDC	3/2	388
GAB/CGC/BGE/FDE/DBD/CAC/BG	3/4	340
CGCD/ECCEF/GGFEFG/E	C/2	306
CGCDEDCB/AFGEG	3/2	365
CGCDE/DDGG/GAGF/G	6/4	530
CGCDEEEF/GAGC	/2	177
CGCD/EFEDBG	6/4	48
G/CGCD/EFEDEF/EFGCDG	6/4	252
C/CGCD/EFEE/DCCB/C	C/2	81
CGCD/EFGE/AGFGE/DC	C/2	93
E/CGCD/EF/GECEDC/D	6/4	382
G/CGCEGFE/DGBDFG	C/2	447
CGCC/AGEDC/CECGE/D	3/4	346
G/CGCG/CBAG	C/2	6
CGCGC/EFGAG	6/4	18

Code	Meter	No.
CGCG/CGEDE/CCCC	/2	308
CGDE/CE/DBBF/DF	C/2	302
CGEA/GCBE/DBAG/G	6/4	179
CGEA/GCDBG/	C/2	219
CGEA/GEDC/CEDB	6/4	123
CG/EA/GEDC/DBAG/C	/2	384
CGEC/GABCDB/CDEDC/	C/2	208
CGECGAG/CGECGCG/	9/4	243
G/CGEDC/AGFEAG	6/4	359
CGED/CDBDCG/AFB	C/2	532
G/CGEDC/DEDBAG	6/8	529
CGEDC/EGA/GECGEC/BD	6/4	418
C/CGEDC/FAGF/EFG	6/4	261
ED/CGEDC/GABCB/ABC	6/4	266
CGEDCG/CBADBAG/	3/2	257
CGED/EFGDEFE	3/4	483
CGE/DG/AFB/GE/FD	C/2	455
CGEE/DEDCBG/CGEE	C/2	456
C/CGEF/GCG/CDCDEF/	6/4	380
C/CGEG/CB/CBCD/E	6/4	210
CGEC/CG/CDCDED	2/2	514
G/CGEGEC/BCDDE/F	6/4	461
CGEGEEGE/CGEFFED	9/4	250
CGFEA/EFGDEFEC/	3/2	353
CGFE/DCBG/	C/2	14
CGFEDC/CGABC/DD	3/2	436
CGFE/DCDEFD/BGCG/	C/2	478
CGF/ED/ECDEF/GFGABG/C	3/4	477
CGFEDE/DECEDEBG	9/4	270
CGF/EFD/CCG/C	3/4	247
G/CGFEG/AGFEDF/G	/2	420
C/CGGA/GEFG/AGFEF	/2	166
CGGAG/FEF/EFGABC	6/4	307
C/CGGC/BAGA/GCAD/BC	C/2	496
CGGEDC/FAGE/	6/4	144
CGGEGABC/BDDEFED/	9/4	408
CGGEGGE/CGGEGABCG	9/4	243
CGGF/EDCD/EGG	C/2	327
C/CGGF/EFGF	6/4	106
CGGF/GABDCB/	6/4	10
CGGF/GAGFD/EEFGE	6/4	247
EF/DCGFE/ABCBAG/AGE	6/4	265
DDDC/BCDG/	6/4	19
DDG/BCDF/ECC	C/2	213
E/DECFD/BGAB/C	6/4	285
DEFECD/GEGE	C/2	50
C/DEFED/EDCGE/	6/4	62
G/ECAGC/BGAB/CBAGEC/D	6/4	516
C/ECAGFEDC/BDDDF	6/4	390
CD/ECBAGAB/CCDEFGA/	3/4	476
E/ECBCD/BABAG	C/2	287
G/ECCCDE/FEDC/	6/4	347
EC/CC/EF/GE/F	3/4	90
ECCC/EFGFE/DBBB/DG	6/4	430
GF/ECCCEGFE/DEFGA	C/2	134
G/ECCD/EA/GAGAGE/F	C/2	370
ECCDE/FBBB/C	C/2	75
E/ECCGCFE/DCBGE/EFDB	C/2	387
G/ECCGE/FFDAG/ECC	6/4	146
ECDAB/CGED	6/4	77
G/ECDB/CBABC/DBCD/B	/2	238
G/ECDCBA/GG/ECCE	C/2	519
D/ECDE/DBD/EFGA/G	C/2	337
ECDEFEDC/DBFED	3/2	427
ECE/BGB/ECEF/GFE	C/2	316
ECE/BGB/GBCBG	/2	151
D/ECECB/GFGC	6/4	453
D/ECEDGD/ECDECDGD/	6/4	395
ECEFG/AFDF/ECCC	/2	480
ECEFGCGC/GCEFGC/	3/2	352
ECEFG/FDDEFG/EC	C/2	55
G/ECEF/GFE/DBDE/F	3/4	272
ECEFG/FEDCB	6/4	160
ECEF/GFGCD/E	6/4	275
GF/ECEG/CDCDE/CGEC	C/2	373
G/ECECG/FDADE/F	6/4	349
C/ECECG/GEA/GAEDFE	6/4	449
ECEGFDB/CCDEGC/BG	C/2	419

Code	Meter	No.
G/ECGB/CG/AGABC/B	C/2	438
D/ECGD/ECDEFD/EAGEDC/C	6/4	460
F/ECGDG/CDCDABCA/B	6/4	443
ECGE/CGGCE/DFEDC	6/4	70
GF/ECGE/FDDA/BG	/2	485
GF/EDCBAG/ABCBC/D	6/4	260
D/EDCBCDB/CC	C/2	334
CD/EDCBC/DBGBAB/CAD	6/4	271
G/EDCBCD/EDEF/GAGECF/	6/4	356
D/EDCB/CDEFGFE/D	C/2	360
CD/EDCBC/DGAG/FED	C/2	220
G/EDCB/CGBA	6/4	331
CD/EDCBG/BDDE/FD	C/2	364
D/EDCCD/EDCCC/BCGC/	6/4	494
EDCC/EGF/EGC/B	3/4	397
EDCCGCCGC/EDCCGCDBD	9/4	502
G/EDCDB/CCC	6/4	117
G/EDCDB/CDEDEF/G	/2	434
G/EDCDBG/CG/EDC	6/4	167
GF/EDCDCB/CCCDE/CCC	6/4	309
ED/CDCBCD/CGF	6/4	174
EDCDEC/DFGB	3/2	290
EDCDEF/GFEBF	6/4	126
GF/EDCEDB/CD/EFE	/2	512
EDCEDC/G/EDCEDC/G	6/4	489
G/EDCEFGE/FGAFG	6/4	255
ED/CEF/GFEDC/BDE/CB/A	C/2	475
G/EDCEG/CE/DEDCB	C/2	262
GF/EDCEGG/CE/DEFEDEC	6/4	414
G/EDCGAB/AAAC/	6/4	228
C/EDC/GC/BAG/	3/4	22
G/EDCGC/BAGDCB	6/4	196
EDC/GCB/CFE/DEDED	3/4	379
G/EDCG/CD/EDEFEDC/D	C/2	452
GF/EDCGC/ECCD/ECDE	C/2	394
D/EDCGFG/AGFED	C2	524
E/EDCGG/DDDD	6/4	88
G/EDEABC/DDD	6/4	405
EDECEFG/FDBCDEDBC/	9/4	291
EDEDCC/DEDCBB/	C/2	28
CD/EDEFEDC/DG	C/2	314
EDEFEDCEFG/ADCBG/E	3/2	425
EDEFG/CGCCD/EEFGFE	C/2	294
G/EDEFG/GAADC/BG/C	6/4	274
EEDC/CDEG/GABBB/	3/2	198
D/EEDC/DDDGF/EDC	6/4	273
EEDC/EFGDC	6/4	1
EEECC/BGAG/ECD	6/4	7
EEE/DCCBC/DDDE/	/2	74
C/EEEDC/DDDG/CCCED/B	6/4	464
EEEDC/DDFED/E	6/4	83
CD/EEEFE/DGFEDED/C	C/2	241
C/EEEFG/FDBBCD/ECC	6/4	244
EEFGFDB/CCDEG	C/2	419
EEFGFGA/GABC	C/2	224
EEG/CEC/ECFE/DCBAG	3/4	361
EEGGEDC/CCEDBAG	C/2	389
D/EEFEDCB/CGCG/FGEEDC/C	6/4	497
EFEFGDG/CDCDEBE/AB	3/4	377
EFGA/BF/DB/	3/4	57
G/EFGAFA/GECEDC/GEGG	6/4	282
C/EFGAG/CBAG	6/4	214
G/EFGAGCBG/EFGAGCD	9/4	446
G/EFGAG/CDBGAB/C	6/4	170
EFGAG/DEFGAFBD/E	3/2	474
GF/EFGAGE/FDEDC/BD	C/2	445
CD/EFGAGF/ECDE/FAABC/B	6/4	231
D/EFGAGFE/EDCCD/EFGAB	C/2	375
CD/EFGAGF/GF/EDCBA/ABAG	6/4	381
G/EFGB/GCBGFE	C/2	428
C/EF/GC/BCD/C	3/4	20
G/EFGCD/BCDGCB/CDEA	6/4	415
EF/GCE/DEDCB/C	C/2	324
G/EFGDC/CCC	6/4	104
G/EFGEAGEC/DGGG/EFGE	/2	500
C/EFGECCECC/EFGECC	9/4	385
C/EFGEDC/DBG	6/4	94
EFGEDC/EDCD	C/2	12

Theme			Theme			Theme		
EFGE/DEC/	3/4	51	GCBAG/ACGFE/FEDEG	6/4	459	GFD/EDCB/CEDEF/	C/2	486
CD/EFGFE/FDGECCD/E	C/2	369	GCBDB/CDECDG/CBAG	6/4	498	GFDE/FEDCBC/	/2	486
C/EF/GFGC/EF/G	C/2	190	GCCA/ADDG/GCCA/EC	C/2	321	GFEA/GCD	C/2	278
C/EFGG/AAAGGG	C2	305	GCC/BCDGBC/G	3/2	444	C/GFED/CBAC/CGEFGE	C/2	431
C/EFGGAG/FGEDEF/EFG	6/4	155	G/GCCCE/DBBDEFF/GG	6/4	292	G/GFEDC/BCDG/G	6/4	63
D/EFGGAGGD/EFGGABC	9/4	233	GCCD/BGG/CBBA/G	6/4	326	GFEDC/CBCG	C/2	58
GF/EFGGC/AAGF/EFGG	C/2	277	C/GCCD/ECCF/FGFDCB	/2	276	GFEDC/DGC/G	C/2	165
EFGGEC/EFGDC	6/4	41	GCCDEDC/DEFGEC	3/2	313	GFEDCGC/GFEFGD	3/2	413
EFGGF/EFEDC	6/4	34	GCCD/EDC/FEDC/DCBAG	C/2	426	GFEDEB/CDEFD	C/2	127
EFGGF/EFGGAB/C	6/4	54	GA/GCCD/EDE/FGFEDECD	C/2	471	GFEDE/FEDCDCB/C	C/2	368
C/EFGGFG/FDDD/DEF	6/4	80	BA/GCD/EDEFEFG/FDFB/D	/2	501	GFEFD/CDB/	6/4	79
EFGGG/EFGGGG	6/4	92	GCEDC/DBG/GCCCD/CDEDCC	3/2	357	A/GFEFDG/ECCE/D	6/4	256
C/EGA/GECBA/BDDD	6/4	283	A/GCEDC/DEDF	6/4	248	GF/EFEDG/CDEFD	C/2	328
C/EGAGEC/EGCADG	9/4	229	C/GCEDC/EGECD	6/4	240	GFEFED/GGGG	6/4	212
C/EGAGEC/FABCDD	9/4	376	GCGE/GEC/ACAF/AFD/	3/4	354	GA/GFEFGA/GDGF/EDC	6/4	268
E/EGAGEDC/CDECD	C/2	515	GDEDE/CDEFEDC/	C/2	472	C/GFEFGC/DCBABG	C/2	450
C/EGBCEG/ABCDBG	6/4	533	GEA/GCD/EFED	C/2	278	C/GFAGFE/FDEG	C/2	482
EG/CBCDBG/ABAC	6/4	216	A/GECBC/DBGAB/CBAG	6/4	225	GFGE/DCBGGA/BAGFE	6/4	207
EGCC/BDGD/ECGC/BDG	/2	495	G/GEC/DEABG/C	6/4	202	EF/GGAGEFD	3/2	124
G/EGCCDE/CGC/CDEEFG	6/4	367	GEC/DEDG/C	3/4	13	GGAGGE/FDFEC/	6/4	61
EGCD/CDCG	C/2	67	A/GECDE/FDDA/GAGEDC/GE	6/4	168	GGCBA/GFE/GECAFD	6/4	470
GF/EGDG/CGCCD/EDCFEFD	/2	491	EF/GECE/DG/EGGE/D	C/2	333	C/GGCC/DBEE/FGED	6/4	120
G/EGECE/GCDD/EFEDEF/D	6/8	462	GECGEC/CAF	6/4	40	GGCD/DEDC/DEDC	6/4	161
EGEDCB/CGCD	6/4	149	GE/DBAG	C/2	5	GGCD/EFGDEF/EGGAB	6/4	103
EGEG/EFGEC/FA	/2	143	GEDC/BCDE/FGAGE/DC	6/4	178	GGCEF/GGCG/	C/2	176
G/EGEGEG/CGFE/FGFED	6/4	399	GEDC/BGF/EFGCG/A	C/2	216	G/GGEC/GAB/CBCD/E	6/4	101
ED/EGFA/DFEG/AGFEFGA/	C/2	378	G/GEDCCG/GAGEG	C/2	504	GGEDE/FEFG	6/4	56
C/EGGA/GFEDG/EC	/2	396	GED/CDEDCDG/GCBA/	3/2	325	GGEE/FEDCBB/C	C/2	65
C/EGGC/GFGAGC/EGGC	C/2	417	A/GED/DFG/ABAGE/DC	6/4	181	C/GGFE/AG/FFED/C	C/2	458
C/EGGEG/ABCAC	6/4	221	G/GEDE/FFDD/GGEF/G	C/2	102	GGFE/DCDEFED/C	C/2	45
EGGEG/DFFDF/EGGEG	6/4	296	A/GEEC/DGA/GEGDC/C	C/2	351	GG/FGEFDC	C/2	69
FED/EFGECG/	C/2	249	C/GEF/DC/DEF/G/AC	3/4	310	EF/GGGAG/FFFGF/EEEFE	6/4	344
FFFED/ECCAB/C	6/4	197	GEFE/DCBAGE/F	C/2	258	GGGE/DEFGEC/FEFG	C/2	503
E/FGAEFG/DEDBAG	6/4	286	EF/GEFG/AEFE/DCDB/G	C/2	169	GGG/EFGG/AGFE/DE/D	C/2	27
GABABC/BCDE/F	C/2	442	G/GEFG/EDC	C/2	2	GGG/EFGG/AGFE/DE/F	C/2	3
G/GAGAB/CCCDC/BAG	6/4	109	G/GEFG/EDECG/G	C/2	71	EF/GGGF/ECFG/A	C/2	36
GAGA/GFEDC	C/2	11	GEFGEF/GFGAGC/GEFG	2/2	526	GGGF/EDCDE/D	C/2	236
G/GAGC/BA/GAGFE/	6/4	91	GEG/CCEDC/DGEG/CCEDC	3/2	154	EF/GGGF/EFGECEC	6/4	236
GAGCD/EDDG/ABCCGE/	C/2	534	GEGCGE/CGCECG	3/4	522	EF/GGGG/AF/GFEDG/	C/2	366
GAGCD/EFEDC	6/4	251	GEGC/GEGC/AFGFE	6/4	164	GGGG/CDECAB/CCCC/	C/2	130
D/GAGEC/EDCB/ABCGEF/D	6/4	230	EF/GEGE/FDEF/G	C/2	35	GGGG/GE/FAGF/CA	/2	82
EF/GAGECE/FGEDEF/G	6/4	203	GEGFDF/ECED	6/4	87	GGGG/GE/FEFG/AF	6/4	52
C/GAGEDC/FABCA/G	6/4	518	GEGFDF/EDCBC/D	6/4	235	EF/GGGG/GEFG/A	6/4	115
G/GAGGAG/GE/FGEDC/C	6/4	158	G/GEGGEG/CBA/GEF	6/4	521	GGGGG/GECEE/F	6/4	72
GCAB/CBAGA/BCBA	C/2	97	G/GEGGEG/GEGGC	6/4	457			
GCBAFB/GFEDEC	6/4	211	GEGG/GEGG	6/4	9			

Index of titles and original spellings

Index entries begin with the title and tune number from this edition, and are followed by the spelling of that title and its page number[1] in the earliest edition of *The Dancing Master* to include it. The spelling or punctuation of a title and its index entry in these original editions often differ; major differences are bracketed in or after the original title. Those differences between the original title and original index entry and other details not included here are: the omission of 'the' in the original indexes; abbreviations in the indexes; full stops at the ends of titles; differences in capitalisation between title and index; the use of brackets for some alternative titles in the original editions; the use of italic as the main typeface in some editions. Italics are used here to indicate that the word (usually a name) was printed in the subsidiary typeface of the original title, whether roman or italic. The following supplements lack indexes: 3A, 6A, 7A, 7B, 7C, 9D, 11A. Surnames are given without the prefix 'Mr' (see p.9).

[1] Or tune number (italicised) in the case of supplements 3A, 3B and 7A, which do not include dance instructions and so have the tunes numbered, several to a page. Tunes with dance instructions are almost all one to a page. Page numbers with asterisks follow Henry Playford's practice in distinguishing those page numbers duplicated in the second edition of Part II (see p.7).

[2] This sign is used in the dance instructions to indicate a repeat

Of noble race was Shinkin 334   Of Noble Race was *Shinkin* 168
Oh! How they frisk it! 236   OH! how they frisk it! *21* [22]
Oil of Barley, The 99   . . . the *Oyle of Barly* 10
Old Abigail's delight 493   Old *Abbigal's* Delight 23
Old bachelor 335   Old *Batchelor* 165
Old Bourrée, The 185   THe old *Bore 57*
Old man is a bed full of bones, An 72   An Old man is a Bed full of bones 76
Old marrinet 186   OLd *Marrinet 48*
Old mole, The 73   The Old Mole 13
Old Noll's jig 494   Old *Nolls* Jigg 7
Old Rigaudon 312   Old (New) Rigadoon 158
Old Simon the King 233   Old *Simon* the King 24 [22]
O mother, Roger 336   O Mother, *Roger* 166
Once I loved a maiden fair 74   Once I loved a Maiden (Mayden) faire 47
On the cold ground 187   ON the cold ground *45*
Open the door to three 113   . . . Open the door to three 110
Opera, The 137   The Op(p)era 157 [159]
Oranges and lemons 128   Orin, ges and Lemons 131
Ormond House 495   *Ormon* House 17

Painted chamber 301   Painted Chamber 1
Pall-mall 253   Pall-Mall 198
Parson's farewell 75   Parsons farewell (farwell) 6
Parson(s) upon Dorothy 107   Parson upon Dorothy 83
Parthenia 24   Parthenia 152
Parthenia 188   P*Arthenia. A Dance 31*
Passepied, A 313   A Paspe 212
Passionate lover(s), The 53   . . . The Passionate Lover 69
Paul's steeple 76   Pauls Steeple 69
Paul's Wharf 77   Pauls Wharfe 86
Pegasus 207   Pegasus 110
Pell-mell 253   Pell-mell 125
Pepper's black 78   Peppers Black 41
Petticoat wag 79   Petticoat wag 68
Phoenix, The 208   The Phenix 112
Piccadilly 66   . . . Pickadilla 78
Picking of sticks 80   Picking of sticks 12
Pilgrim, The 462   The Pillgrim (Pilgrim) 272
Pool's hole 314   *Pool's* hole (Pools Hole) 214
Pope Joan 337   Pope *Joan* 181
Pope's Jig, The 394   The Pope's Jigg (Dr. *Pope's* Jigg) 58
Porter's dream 158   POrters Dream *54*
Porter's lamentation 159   POrters Lamentation *45*
Portsmouth 463   Portsmouth (*Portsmouth*) 243
Pretty miss 315   Pretty Miss 219
Prince George 254   Prince George 195
Prince George's March 284   PRince *George's* March 31 [32]
Prince Rupert's March 81   Prince Ruperts March 55 [57]
Princes(s), The 464   The Princess (Princes) 281
Princess's court, The 496   The Princesse's Court 1
Private wedding, The 419   . . . the private Wedding 301
Puddings and pies 406   Puddings (Pudding) and Pies 210
Punch bowl, The 465   The Punch-Bow(l) 302
Punk's delight (the new way), The 82   The Punks Delight *the new way* 27 [72]
Purlongs, The 365   The Purlongs 18
Putney Ferry 209   Putney Ferry 88
Put on thy smock on a Monday 210   Put on thy Smock a Munday (Put on thy smock on Monday) 90
Pye Corner 338   Pye-corner 164

Quaker's grace, The 528   . . . The Quaker(s) Grace 357
Queen's birthday, The 514   The Queen's birthday 338
Queen's delight, The 189   THe Queens Delight 64
Queen's delight, The 527   The Queen's Delight 363
Queen's Head, The 497   The Queens Head 21
Queen's Jig, The 466   The Queens Jigg 260

Rake's delight, The 527   The Rake's delight 202
Red bull, The 407   The red Bull 209
Red House 339   Red-House 177
Reeve's maggot 467   *Reeve's* Magott (Maggot) 263
Resolution, The 528   The Resolution 357
Richmond Ball 328   *Richmond* Ball 211
Richmond Green 285   RIchmond-Green *14* [15]
Rigaudon 305   Rigadoon 4
Rigaudon 312   Rigadoon 158
Rigaudon 330   Rigadoon 187
Rockingham Castle 340   *Rockingham* Castle 188
Roger of Coverly 341   *Roger of Coverly* 167
Rose is white and rose is red 83   Rose is white and Rose is red (Rose is red, and Rose is white) 37
Round, The 468   The Round 282
Round O 512   Round O 354
Round Robin 286   ROund Robin *23* [24]
Row well, ye marriners 84   Row well ye Marriners 102
Royal Navy, The 515   The Royal Navy 348
Rub her down with straw 469   Rub her down with Straw 307
Rufty tufty 85   Rufty(,) tufty 70
Rummer, The 255   The Rummer 189
Running Bourrée, The 190   THe Running (Runing) Bore *50*
Russel, The 529   The *Russel* 356

Sage leaf 211   Sage Leaf 18
Sailor's delight 399   The Saylors delight 37
St. Albans 470   St. *Albans* 259
St. Catherine 471   St. *Catherine* 288
St. Dunstan 287   ST. Dunstan *22* [23]
St. Martin's 86   Saint Martins 66
St. Martin's Lane 366   St. Martin's (*Martin's*) Lane 5
St. Paul's steeple 76   St. *Paul's* Steeple (*Paul's* Steeple) 43
Sancho Pancho 342   Sancho-Pancho 162
Saraband, The 87   The Saraband 17
Saturday night and Sunday morn 88   Saturday night and Sunday morn 80
Sawney and Jockey 234   Sawney *and* Jockey 9
Sawney was tall 234   *Sawney* was tall 96
Scotch air 508   *Scotch* Ayre 347
Scotch cap 89   Scotch Cap 99
Scotch Firk, A 160   A Scotch Firke *48*
Scotchman's dance, in 'The northern lass' 288   THe Scotch-man's Dance in the *Northern Lass* 29 [30]
Scotland 408   *Scotland* 202
Scots Rant 161   SCots Rant *56*
Sedany, The 90   Sedanny (Sedany) 71
Sellenger's Round 129   Sellengers Round 132
Serag's Hornpipe, The 535   The *Serag's* Hornpipe 148
Shaking of the sheets, The 70   . . . The shaking of the Sheets 75
Sham doctor, The 388   The sham Doctor 26*
Shepherdess, The 20   . . . the Shepherdess 38
Shepherd's daughter, The 107   The Shepherds Daughter 81
Shepherds' holiday 91   Shepheards Holyday 101
Shore's trumpet tune 389   *Shores* (Shores) Trumpet Tune 34*

Short's Garden(s) 256   Short's Garden 201
Siege of Buda, The 306   The Siege of *Buda* 3
Siege of Limerick, The 343   Siege of *Limerick* 173
Silver faulken, The 108   The Silver Faulken 112
Simeron's dance, The 191   THe Simerons Dance 33
Simple Simon 130   Simple Simon 114
Singleton's slip 192   SIngleton's Slip (Slipp) *40*
Sion House 257   Sion-House 187
Sir Foplin 289   SIr Foplin *15* [16]
Sir Nicholas Culley 18   . . . Sir *Nicholas Cull(e)y* 35
Sir Roger 93   (. . . Sir *Roger*) 129
Skellamefago 92   Skellamefago (Skellamfago) 34
Slaughterhouse 498   Slaughter House 4
Slip, The 93   The Slip 104
Smith's new Rant 131   *Smith's* new Rant 20
Smith's Rant 131   Smiths Rant 119
Soldier and the sailor, The *or* A soldier and a sailor 367   The Soldier and the Sailer 7
Soldier's life, A 94   Souldiers Life 65
Solomon's Jig 109   Solomons Jigge (Jegg) 98
Spaniard, The 95   The Spanyard 36
Spanish gipsy, The 96   The Spanish Jeepsie (Jepsies) 23
Spanish Jig 344   Spanish Jigg 171
Sparagus garden, The 126   . . . the Sparaguss (-) Garden 124
Spring Garden 132   Spring Garden 115
Staggins's Jig 235   Mr. *Staging's* Jigg 4
Stanes Morris 97   Stanes Morris 87
Step stately 98   Step Stately 100
Stingo 99   Stingo 10
Strawberries and cream 121   . . . Strawber(r)ies and Cream 122
Summer's day, A 101   . . . a Summers day 107
Sweet Kate 212   Sweet Kate 94
Sweet William 219   . . . Sweet *William* 13
Sword dance, The 499   The Sword Dance 16
Symphony, The 5   . . . the Simphony 73

Tailor's daugher, The 79   . . . The Taylors Daughter 80 [82]
Take not a woman's anger ill 368   Take not a Woman's Anger ill, For if one won't, another will 9
Taylor's trip 472   Taylors Tripp 312
Temple, The 473   The Temple (*Temple*) 274
Temple Change, The 390   The *Temple-Change* (Temple Change) 28*
Ten pound lass 213   Ten Pound Lass 150
Thomas you cannot 214   Thomas you Cannot 93
Three sheep skins 409   Three Ship Skins (Sheep-skins) 215
Throw the house out of the window 162   THrow the House out of the Windowe *33*
Tiger, The 474   The Tyger (*Tyger*) 246
Tom Tinker 100   Tom Tinker 88
Touch and go 475   Touch and Go 277
Touch and take 110   Tutch and take 102
Trenchmore 111   Trenchmore 103
Trip to Bury, A 500   A trip to Bury 18
Trip to St. John's Court, A 532   A Trip to St. *John's* Court 358
Trip to the Jubilee, as 'tis danc'd at the play-house, The 376   The trip to the *Jubilee*, as 'tis danc'd at the Play-House 289
Tunbridge Walks 516   *Tunbridge* Walks 352
Turnham Green 218   TUrnham-Green *6* [7]
'Twas within a furlong of Edinburgh Town 369   'Twas within a Furlong of *Edinborough* Town 21
Twelfth eve 501   Twelfe Eve 14
Twenty-ninth of May, The 258   The *29th of May* (Twenty-ninth of May) 207
Twins, The 133   The Twins 112
Tythe pig 345   Tythe Pig 190